Praise for *Learning Leadership*

"How heartening it is to see definitive proof that great leaders are made, not born. Learn for yourself how to make critical connections, collect, and use constructive feedback, and lead any size organization with deliberation and success with the wisdom mined, analyzed, and presented by Kouzes and Posner!"

—**Marshall Goldsmith**, #1 *New York Times*
Bestselling Author of *Triggers, MOJO,*
and *What Got You Here Won't Get You There*

"So, you want to be a leader? This book shows you how. With fluid writing, comprehensive research, and actionable insights, Kouzes and Posner debunk myths and demonstrate that leadership is comprised of a clear set of skills and abilities that can be learned, practiced, and mastered."

—**Tina Seelig**, Professor of the Practice, Stanford School of
Engineering; Author of *Insight Out, inGenius*, and
What I Wish I Knew When I Was 20

"Kouzes and Posner believe, as I do, that leaders are made, and they support that belief with hard evidence and live examples. *Learning Leadership* is rich with essential tools and practical advice for becoming an extraordinary leader in any environment. This is the book you need to come out on top!"

—**John C. Maxwell**, *New York Times*
Bestselling Author and Leadership Expert

"*Learning Leadership* covers the fundamentals of what it takes to become an exemplary leader. Kouzes and Posner have done a wonderful job recognizing and sharing the mindset of leaders as learners—and they offer evidence-based tools and techniques that you can put to use right away."

—**Adam Grant**, Wharton Professor;
New York Times Bestselling Author of *Give and Take* and *Originals*

"In my work, people often ask, 'Is there one best book you could recommend on leadership?' In the past, that choice was difficult, but not anymore. *Learning Leadership* is that one book with widespread appeal and true value. This book gives each of us the ability to set upon a lifelong path of development as leaders."

—**Tom Kolditz**, Executive Director, Doerr Institute for New Leaders,
Rice University; Brigadier General, U.S. Army (ret);
Professor Emeritus, Behavioral Sciences and Leadership, West Point

"Jim Kouzes and Barry Posner have delivered (yet again!) with *Learning Leadership*. This relevant and engaging book powerfully demonstrates how leadership is, in fact, a learnable competency. It gives readers a useful framework on how to become a leader, and how to learn and grow as a leader. A wonderful blend of deep insight coupled with immediately practical application, *Learning Leadership* is indispensable to any current or aspiring leader."

—**Stephen M. R. Covey**, *New York Times* Bestselling
Author of *The Speed of Trust*, and Coauthor of *Smart Trust*

"Kouzes and Posner have done it again. Recognizing the dynamic leadership challenges of the twenty-first century, they have created an essential leadership text that helps aspiring leaders lift their game in an ambitious but practical fashion."

—**Doug Conant**, Chairman, Avon Products;
Former CEO, Campbell Soup Company; Founder and CEO,
ConantLeadership; Chairman, Kellogg Executive Leadership Institute

"A compelling and practical read from two of the most trusted thinkers in the field, *Learning Leadership* is a road map to becoming the best leader you can be."

—**Chip Conley**, *New York Times* Bestselling Author of
Emotional Equations; Head of Global Hospitality and Strategy, AirBnB

"*Learning Leadership* is an excellent guidebook for those who are newer to leadership and the concepts and design also lend themselves to the continuous practice of the seasoned leader as well. I appreciate the concept of the leadership journal and self-coaching actions shared at the end of each chapter as they guide the reader in reflection and practice."

—**Katya Armistead**, Dean of Student Life,
University of California, Santa Barbara

"In this wonderful book, Kouzes and Posner have summarized, in a highly engaging and accessible way, the very best lessons from irrefutable research about how to become the best leader you can possibly be. I wish I had it available 30 years ago: I would have recommended it to every single job candidate, as I will do from now on."

—**Claudio Fernández-Aráoz**, Senior Advisor,
Egon Zehnder; Author of *It's Not the
How or the What But the Who*

"Discover your inner leader. Embrace that everyone has leadership potential. Use the resources and practices in this book to tap your inner leader. For young and emerging leaders this is the book for learning leadership and empowering others."

—**Juana Bordas**, Bestselling Author of Award-Winning Book *Salsa, Soul, and Spirit: Leadership for a Multicultural Age*

"We all talk about leadership as a journey and I believe Jim Kouzes and Barry Posner just provided us with the map. Cover to cover *Learning Leadership: The Five Fundamentals of Becoming an Exemplary Leader* is exceptional and should become required reading for every leader regardless of their age or experience. A sincere thank you to Jim and Barry for their lifelong commitment to bringing out the leader in all of us."

—**Mark Fernandes**, Chief Leadership Officer, Luck Companies

"Hugely inspiring and motivating. Kouzes and Posner show how people at every level can develop as leaders from the inside out by identifying what they uniquely have to bring to their organization, team, or community—proactively, without waiting to be singled out. *Learning Leadership* affirms that every one of us can all make, not just a difference, but also the particular difference we want to make in the world. This is a wonderful and important book."

—**Sally Helgesen**, Author of *The Female Vision*, *The Web of Inclusion*, and *The Female Advantage*

"Every emerging leader needs a great vivid picture of what great leadership looks like. They have a lifetime to mold and shape their future. Jim and Barry provide the map and the landmarks for this crucial leadership journey. They certainly have the background and experience to be the Sherpas!"

—**Beverly Kaye**, Founder, Career Systems International; Coauthor of *Love 'Em or Lose 'Em: Getting Good People to Stay* and *Hello Stay Interviews, Goodbye Talent Loss*

"*Learning Leadership* is a practical and wonderful road map for anyone in leadership considering leadership or afraid they were not good enough for leadership. Jim and Barry challenge and motivate the reader every step of the way to reach inside for the latent capabilities for great leadership. The research and case studies are undeniable proof that there is opportunity for greatness in each and every one of us."

—**Kory Kogon**, Global Productivity Practice Leader, Franklin Covey; Coauthor of *The 5 Choices: The Path to Extraordinary Productivity*

"*Learning Leadership* captures the essence of being lifelong learners striving to be the best that one can be. The big ideas in this book reaffirm why effective leaders, both students and educators, must be learning leaders and why they inspire engagement, make a difference, and must believe in themselves as having the power and capacity to be exemplary. *Learning Leadership* will no doubt be the valuable foundational resource that will fuel my leadership work for the next decade."

—**Wendy Lim**, Assistant Superintendent of Schools, Richmond, British Columbia, Canada

"Jim and Barry's insightful book reminds young professionals that their education does not stop with graduation. They must continue to learn, to practice, and to develop as leaders, and the five fundamental lessons of leadership in the book guide and inspire this new generation into becoming the leaders of tomorrow."

—**Susan Luchey**, Leadership and Career Consultant; Directs Leadership Program, University of Delaware

"The conversational and optimistic tone of *Learning Leadership* belies the serious leadership culture shift that Kouzes and Posner highlight in this rich addition to the leadership bookshelf. Readers are invited to evaluate their capacity to lead—and that of those around them—in the context of upending the social belief that only certain individuals 'belong' in the leadership pipeline. The growth-and-the-greater-good mindset the authors emphasize for preparing everyone to lead is an easy and welcome mantra to embrace. The earlier this philosophy can be introduced to young adults and their mentors, the better; and *Learning Leadership* is an excellent springboard."

—**Mariam G. MacGregor**, Professional Development Center, Neeley School of Business, Texas Christian University; Author of the Award-Winning *Building Everyday Leadership* curriculum

"In a leadership development space that is often full of sizzle and 'revolutionary' new ideas that lack real substance, Kouzes and Posner offer sound advice that is incredibly valuable for emerging leaders and existing leaders looking to sharpen their skills alike. Kouzes and Posner offer a perfect combination of hard facts and analysis derived from deep research and anecdotes that are both practical and relatable. They don't focus on the one-in-a-billion success stories of celebrity entrepreneurs and business people that are often rooted in inapplicable circumstance—instead they make leadership development tangible, sharing stories from everyday people, making their sage advice more achievable. Each chapter's Self-Coaching Actions bring their core leadership principles to life, leading you to not only think through how each applies to you, but also to implement what you have learned."

—**Aaron McDaniel**, Millennial Expert, Speaker, Entrepreneur; Author of *The Young Professional's Guide* Series

"It's time to stop looking outside for answers, to wake up to the divine brilliance that each of us represents. Life is too short to be a follower of someone else's dream, to keep playing small by giving away our power. It's up to each of us to lead, to smash through the threshold of fear and to rise up and make our mark in our own unique way. With *Learning Leadership*, Jim Kouzes and Barry Posner have created an excellent road map to help us on this journey, offering practical tips and examples to help you realize your innate greatness."

—**Ruairí McKiernan**, Award-Winning Social Entrepreneur and Presidential Appointee to Ireland's Council of State

"How many times do people get told they simply 'aren't a leader'? More often than not, it's because there's one mold that we're trying to fit people into. But leadership comes in all shapes and forms, and needs this multitude. It needs the onlyness—that unique perspective born of your history and experience visions and hopes that only you can bring. This book shows you how."

—**Nilofer Merchant**, Former Apple and High-Tech Executive and Entrepreneur; Winner of Thinkers50 Award of Future Thinkers; the number one person in the world most likely to influence the future of management in both theory and practice.

"It has always been valuable to bring Jim and Barry's work to my students and young leaders. With *Learning Leadership*, they continue to impress, giving new insights, captivating stories, and practical tips, ultimately revitalizing our perceptions of what it means to be a leader, helping others to grow and to learn, and discover exactly what leadership is and how to achieve it."

—**Bill Shannon**, Former Executive, Duke Clinical Research Institute

"*Learning Leadership* is another jewel from leadership gurus Kouzes and Posner. Whether you are a new leader or have many years of experience, I guarantee you will find valuable development ideas for you and your organization in this book."

—**Steve Skarke**, President, The Kaneka Foundation

"*Learning Leadership* is like having your own personal leadership coach. Or make that coaches. Top leadership thinkers Jim Kouzes and Barry Posner distill thirty years of hands-on research into a book so filled with practical tips that you're guaranteed to become a better leader. "

—**Bill Treasurer**, CEO, Giant Leap Consulting;
Author of *Leaders Open Doors*

LEARNING
LEADERSHIP

THE FIVE FUNDAMENTALS OF BECOMING
AN EXEMPLARY LEADER

JAMES M. KOUZES
BARRY Z. POSNER

WILEY

ISBN 978-1-119-14428-1 (Hardcover)
ISBN 978-1-119-14429-8 (ePDF)
ISBN 978-1-119-14430-4 (ePub)

Printed in the United States of America

10 9 8 7 6 5 4 3 2

We gratefully dedicate this book to Travis Carrigan, Amanda Crowell, Abigail Donahue, Garrett Jensen, Amelia Klawon, David Klawon, Armeen Komeili, Nicholas Lopez, Amanda Posner, and William J. Stribling. These leaders reviewed this book in various draft stages, providing feedback, raising questions, sharing experiences, and offering insights. They kept us focused on leadership— on the skills and behaviors accessible to anyone who wants to learn about becoming, and being, more effective— regardless of his or her position, role, time, or place.

CONTENTS

THE WORLD NEEDS EXEMPLARY LEADERS

There's a leadership shortage in the world. It's not a shortage of potential talent. The people are out there. The eagerness is out there. The resources are out there. The capability is out there.

The shortage is a result of three primary factors: demographic shifts, insufficient training and experiences, and the prevailing mindsets that discourage people from learning to lead.

Currently 25 percent of the global workforce comprises millennials (those born between 1981 and 1997), and in some countries that number approaches 50 percent.[1] By 2025 estimates are that millennials will comprise 75 percent of the global workforce. At the same time as their numbers in the workplace are growing daily, organizations around the world do not feel that they have an ample leadership pipeline to meet present and future needs.[2] An alarming 86 percent of respondents to the latest World Economic Forum survey think there is a *leadership crisis* in the world today,[3] and most companies are *seriously worried* about their leadership bench strength.[4] The demographic shifts are simply creating demand for exemplary leadership that exceeds supply.[5]

If the need for leadership development is great, then why is the pipeline nearly empty? Part of the answer comes from research conducted by leadership scholar Jack Zenger. He looked at his worldwide database of people participating in leadership training and found that their average age was 42. However, the average age of supervisors in the database was 33. "It follows then," Jack reports, "that if they're not entering leadership training programs until they're 42, they are getting no leadership training at all as supervisors. And they're operating with the company untrained, on average, for over a decade."[6] Wow!

Let us ask you something: Would you seek medical treatment from an untrained physician? Would you allow an untrained accountant to audit your company's books? Or, would you hire an untrained engineer to design a new self-driving car? Of course you wouldn't. So, why is this permitted with leaders?

Here's another sobering fact to add to this shortage of leadership and inadequate preparation. There has been a global decline in the level of trust that people have in their leaders. According to the Edelman Trust Barometer—a highly respected annual study of trust in major institutions and their leaders—"the number of countries with trusted institutions has fallen to an all-time low among the informed public. Among the general population, the trust deficit is even more pronounced, with nearly two-thirds of countries falling into the distruster category."[7] Around the world people trust their leaders less and less—no wonder there is a leadership crisis.

For all the talk about the importance of leadership development and the need for better leaders, organizations—including governments and schools—have been putting little of their money where their mouths are. They haven't been doing what they say is vitally important. This is a somber global concern. At the same time, it is a huge opportunity for those organizations and individuals who choose to take the initiative.

It's this opportunity that motivated us to write this book. We've been researching and writing about leadership for three and a half decades, and we've been developing leaders for even longer. But we're seeing a growing divide between demand and supply that needs to be filled—and filled rapidly. We want to continue contributing not only to narrowing that chasm but also to supporting the initiative to create more and better leaders for the world.

THE LEADERSHIP MINDSET

In seminars we've been asking participants this question: "How many of you think of yourself as a leader?" In a group of 50 people, typically only six raise their hands. Even though these are usually people who have come together for leadership development, only about 10 percent identify themselves as leaders. Perhaps people are being modest and they think that if they say they're leaders they'll appear arrogant and as braggadocios. Maybe. But we think there's more to it than that. A mythology about leadership persists that makes people reluctant to claim leadership for themselves. It's as if leadership starts with a capital *L* and is reserved only for those with some special talent, birthright, gene, calling, position, or title. This perspective creates an invisible barrier and is a limiting belief that stops many from answering the call.

Debi Coleman is one of the first leaders we ever interviewed about personal-best leadership practices and the first leader we quoted in the very first edition of our book *The Leadership Challenge*. At that time Debi was vice president of worldwide manufacturing for Apple Computers. In our interview she explained, "I think good people deserve good leadership. The people I manage deserve the best leadership in the world."[8] Debi is now managing partner of SmartForest Ventures, a venture capital firm, and serves on numerous boards. When we caught up with her again, we learned that her perspective on leadership is the same today as when we first talked with her more than 30 years ago.

Debi expresses the spirit of all exemplary leaders. They strive mightily to deliver the best leadership in the world because they firmly believe that people deserve it. Most likely that's exactly what you want from your leaders. If you believe that the people you now lead, or will lead in the future, deserve the best leadership in the world and if it's clear that there's a growing need for an increased quantity and quality of leaders, then it is imperative that you become the best leader you can be. Step one is to develop a leadership mindset. You don't have to wait for an organization to offer a program for you to become the best. Nor do you have to wait for someone else to give you permission or provide some special resource. Just as Dorothy and her colleagues in *The Wizard of Oz* discovered, you already have everything you need to become an exemplary leader.

This is the other reason why we wrote this book. We want to address and rectify some prevailing myths and misconceptions about what it takes to *learn to become* an exemplary leader.

LEARNING TO BECOME AN EXEMPLARY LEADER

After more than 30 years of research, we know that *you* are fully capable of leading. You may not realize it or fully believe it, but it's true. It's also true for 99.999 percent of people in the world. (That's a statistic we'll explain in one of the early chapters.) The larger purpose of this book is to share with you what we've learned about how you can create the conditions, inside yourself and in the context in which you live and work, to become a much better leader than you are today.

We show that you can learn to be a better leader than you are today if you believe in yourself, aspire to be great, challenge yourself to grow, engage the support of others, and practice deliberately. In each of the chapters of this book, we share a key message about developing exemplary leadership, and we offer a practical tip on how to increase your capacity to lead.

Learning Leadership is divided into seven parts. Part I is on the fundamentals. It sets the tone for the book and provides the context for discussing what people need to do to become better leaders. We talk about the myths and assumptions that inhibit leadership development, the five fundamentals of becoming an exemplary leader, the evidence that leadership matters, and how you are already leading but not frequently enough.

In Part II of *Learning Leadership*, we discuss the essential elements of the first fundamental: Believe you can. We stress how important it is to have a strong belief in your capabilities and a mindset that leadership can be learned. We present evidence that learning is the master skill and that leadership emerges from within.

Part III is about the second fundamental: Aspire to excel. This part of the book talks about the importance of knowing who you are and knowing what is important to you. You can't lead others if you don't know yourself. You also have to be concerned about the future. Who you are today is not who you will be in the future, and the same is true for your constituents. We also point out that leadership is a relationship and not simply about the leader's personal aspirations. Leadership requires you to know and appreciate your constituents.

Part IV addresses the third fundamental of becoming an exemplary leader: Challenge yourself. This part of the book discusses how challenge is critical to learning. You need to take initiative in your own development. We point out that there will be inevitable setbacks and failures along the way that require grit, courage, and resilience to persist in learning and becoming the best you can be.

Part V is about the fourth fundamental: Engage support. Here we point out that everyone who achieves excellence gets support and coaching along the way. Whether it's family, managers at work, or professional coaches, leaders need the advice and counsel and the care and support of others. To learn leadership, you need to get connected to a network of resources. You also need feedback to know what progress you are making, how you are growing, and what you still need to be working on.

The fifth fundamental, practice deliberately, is the focus of Part VI. In this part we talk about the fact that to become great at leadership, you have to spend time practicing the skills. Just being in the role of a leader is insufficient. You have to set goals, participate in designed learning experiences, ask for feedback, and get coaching. You also have to put in the time every day and make learning leadership a daily habit.

Part VII of *Learning Leadership* is on the will and the way. We conclude the book with a chapter that summarizes the key messages and offers commentary on how it's essential to follow through on your commitments to learn. The proof is in the doing, not in the deciding to do. We also stress how critical it is for leaders to be positive, energetic, and hopeful. In tough times these are vital ingredients in becoming exemplary.

WHO SHOULD READ THIS BOOK

As we wrote this book we kept the emerging leaders in the forefront of our minds—those who aspire to a leadership role, those who are just beginning to supervise others, and those who must necessarily influence and work with other people to accomplish their objectives. We want *Learning Leadership* to be a guide you can use as you develop your self-concept as a leader and your ideas about what leadership means. We wanted to provide a framework that would help you create a context as well as foster a set of beliefs conducive to your growth and development.

In addition, *Learning Leadership* will be of great value to leadership developers, internal and external trainers, and coaches who are focused on building the next generation of leaders in their client organizations—as well as those who have a responsibility and need to help people be the best they can be. This includes supervisors and managers at all levels. The next generations of leaders need your wisdom and experience if they are going to excel and take your organizations to the next level.

According to recent studies, more than 50 percent of young people want to become leaders in their organizations, although they don't necessarily view *organization* in a traditional way. We know that they also seek challenging assignments and are willing to work hard but that their greatest fear is that there's a "lack of professional growth opportunity" in too many of their organizations.[9] Their willingness to stick around may well be contingent upon how well leadership developers and managers respond to this need.

HOW TO USE THIS BOOK

We want you to *use Learning Leadership* and not just read it. To that end, we've divided the book into short, bite-sized chapters. Read during a train ride to work, while taking a break in your day, or in the evening when you want to spend some time thinking about how you will enhance your leadership capabilities. Also, in each of the chapters that follow, there is a self-coaching action. It's something you can do in a few minutes right then, but you may want to return to these later when you have more time. For most of these actions, we strongly recommend you create a leadership journal. Journaling has been shown to be one of the most effective learning tools and significantly helps you embed the learning you derive from each chapter. Your journal can be just a spiral-bound notebook, something fancier, or an electronic file in your tablet or desktop. It'll be a place to store your reflections, responses, experiences, and lessons learned. And keep it handy. We have a feeling that you'll want to refer to it again and again.

Early reviewers of this book have told us that there's a lot to do here. We agree. It can seem quite daunting. As with learning any set of skills, you must constantly practice if you want to improve. There's no such thing as instant expertise. Putting these concepts into practice takes time, and for exemplary leaders, they believe that it's a lifelong learning journey.

Go at your own pace. People have different learning styles. You might want to read the entire text and then go back and do the self-coaching actions. You may want to take a section at a time and read it over a period of weeks or even months. You might want to do the coaching activities chapter by chapter. Use the ideas in this book in whatever way works for you. The point is that learning leadership requires practice, practice takes time, and you can learn to be a better leader than you are today.

Finally, give yourself a bit of grace. If you are serious about becoming a better leader, and willing to put in the time and effort, then don't forget to take care of yourself. Pace yourself. You can't build muscle strength all at once; rest between exercises is necessary. Similarly, every suggestion you have for yourself, or others, will not be spot-on the first time. There will be setbacks.

Make sure you build an internal, possibly even external, support system that can get you through the inescapable missteps and disappointments along the leadership journey. You may lose some battles, but keep your eye on the bigger picture.

The world needs exemplary leaders. And it needs exemplary leaders at all levels and in all functions. Your constituents, as well as your colleagues, need you to become the best leader you can be. They need you to lead with your best self. They need you to become an exemplary leader not only for today; they need you to be exemplary tomorrow and into the future. We hope this book will be stimulating and informative on your journey to becoming an exemplary leader.

James M. Kouzes
Orinda, California

Barry Z. Posner
Berkeley, California

April 2016

PART I

LEARNING LEADERSHIP FUNDAMENTALS

L eadership potential isn't something that some people have and other people don't. It's much more broadly distributed than traditionally accepted views suggest. You already have the capacity to lead, but some prevailing myths and assumptions about leadership get in the way of your becoming the best leader you can be. To become an exemplary leader, you have to move past the myths and get down to applying the fundamentals that will enable you to learn and grow as a leader.

Leadership is essential because it makes a significant difference in people's levels of engagement, commitment, and performance. Developing your leadership capabilities will help you improve the way people around you feel about their workplace and promote more productive organizations. Learning to be a better leader also enhances your feelings of self-worth and meaningfulness.

Our research shows that a universal set of leadership practices is associated with exemplary leadership, and these practices are within the capacity of everyone to follow. The challenge is to increase the frequency with which you engage in these leadership practices and become more comfortable and confident in their use.

In the next three chapters we take a look at these key themes on becoming an exemplary leader:

- Leaders are born and so are you.
- Leadership makes a difference.
- You are already leading, just not frequently enough.

CHAPTER 1

LEADERS ARE BORN AND SO ARE YOU

We've been writing and speaking about exemplary leadership for more than 30 years, and throughout that time there's one question people ask us more often than any other. That most frequently asked question is some variation of "Are leaders born or made?" Maybe you're wondering the same thing.

Our answer to that question has always been the same: We have never met a leader who was not born. We've also never met an accountant, artist, athlete, engineer, lawyer, physician, scientist, teacher, writer, or zoologist who was not born.

You might be thinking, "Well that's not fair. That's a trick question. Everyone is born." That's precisely our point. Every one of us is born, and every one of us has the necessary material to become a leader—including you. The question you should be asking yourself is not "Will I make a difference?" In becoming a better leader, the more demanding and significant question you should be asking is "How will I make the difference I want?"

And just for the record, no one has ever asked us, "Are managers born or made?"

Let's get something straight right from the start. Leadership is not some mystical quality that only a few people have and everyone else doesn't. Leadership is not preordained. Neither is it the private reserve of a special class of charismatic men and women. Leadership is not a gene. It is not a trait. There is just no hard evidence to suggest that leadership is imprinted in the DNA of some people and not others.

We've collected assessment data from millions of people around the world. We can tell you without a doubt that there are leaders in every profession, every type of organization, every religion, and every country, from young to old, male and female. It's a myth that leadership can't be learned—that you either have it, or you don't. There is leadership potential everywhere we look.

Asking, "Are leaders born or made?" is not a very productive question. It's the old nature versus nurture argument, and it doesn't get at a more important question that must be asked and answered. The more useful question is "Can you, and those you work with, become better leaders than you are today?" The answer to that question is a resounding yes.

There are people who maintain that not everyone has the potential to lead and not everyone has the capacity to learn to lead. That's because myths, misconceptions, and false assumptions about leadership create barriers to developing leaders at all levels. One of the first challenges on the path to exemplary leadership is to overcome these folk legends and false assumptions. They foster a model of leadership that is antithetical to the way real-life leaders operate. They also create unnecessary barriers to the revitalization of our organizations and communities.

Before we can examine evidence and examples of the mindsets that enable people just like you to become the best leaders they can be, we need to address some of the fables that keep people from thinking that they can provide leadership and be leaders. Five myths inhibit learning to lead and contribute most to the misunderstandings about what leadership is and isn't.

THE TALENT MYTH

The talent myth has captivated the training and development world for years, and some have come to accept it as the new gospel. If only you search far and wide, and long and hard, you'll be able to identify the best and the brightest people and then place them in all the existing leadership roles. Problem solved. No training required; just find the right person. Well, good luck with that.

Talent is overrated.[1] Florida State University professor and noted authority on expertise K. Anders Ericsson and his colleagues have found, over the 30 years of their research, that raw talent is not all there is to becoming a top performer. It doesn't matter whether it's in sports, music, medicine, computer programming, mathematics, or other fields; talent is not the key that unlocks excellence.[2] In studying what it takes to succeed and how people reach their goals, Professor Heidi Grant Halvorson at Columbia Business School reaches a similar conclusion, arguing that the emphasis on talent, smarts, and innate ability has done more harm than good.[3] As she points out, there's a vast difference between "being good" and "getting better."

Leadership is not a talent that you have or you don't. In fact, it is not *a talent* but an observable, learnable set of skills and abilities. Leadership is distributed in the population like any other set of skills.

For more than three decades we have been fortunate to study the stories of thousands of ordinary people who have led others to make extraordinary things happen.[4] There are millions more stories and examples. The belief that leadership is available only to a talented few is a far more powerful deterrent to development than anything else is. It prevents too many people from even trying, let alone excelling.

To become a better leader than you are right now, the first fundamental thing you have to do is to *believe you can* be a better leader and that you can learn to improve your leadership skills and abilities. Without that belief, there's no training or coaching that's going to do much good.

THE POSITION MYTH

This myth associates leadership with a hierarchal position. It assumes that when you have a position at the top, you're automatically a leader. It assumes that leadership is a title and that if you don't have a title of authority, you aren't a leader. It assumes that leadership starts with a capital *L*.

Every day, the mass media and social media perpetuate this myth. People write and talk about how the recent turnaround of an organization was because of what *the* chief executive officer (CEO) did or that *the* founder of a new start-up was responsible for a multibillion-dollar valuation. It's as if people at the top, or those with the highest rank and the most privilege, are the only ones who ever do anything extraordinary. Nonsense.

Nothing could be further from the truth. Leadership is not a rank, a title, or a place. Look it up in the dictionary. You'll find that leadership starts with a lowercase *l*.[5] And the word *lead* literally comes from an Old English word meaning "to go" or "to guide." That's what leadership is about: going places and guiding others. You could be a CEO, but it's much more likely that you are a parent, coach, teacher, frontline worker, middle manager, volunteer, community activist, or concerned citizen. Every student of history knows that world-changing movements have been initiated and led by people without title, rank, or tenure.

It's also true that those who made it to the top didn't start there. More than likely, they got there because they learned leadership skills along the way. Again, you don't have to be at the top to lead; you can lead from any direction. Leadership is much more about what you do than it is about where you are sitting.

Leading is about the actions you take, not the position you hold. It's about the values that guide your decisions and actions. It's about the visions you have for yourself and others. To become an exemplary leader, the second fundamental is that you have to *aspire to excel*. You have to aim for something greater, dream of something better, and strive for something nobler than what exists right now. You have principles that guide you and that transform and lift people up to become their best selves.

THE STRENGTHS MYTH

From the ancient literature on leadership that searched for the individual kissed by the gods (charisma) to historical great man approaches (already limited by gender biases), people have been searching for a formula or magic elixir that explains leadership success. The current fascination is with the concept of *strengths*.

Now there's nothing inherently wrong with the notion that there are certain skills, knowledge, and attitudes that produce higher levels of performance in a task, whether it's sales, engineering, nursing, or hospitality. Leadership is required of all professions, and it has its own set of skills and abilities. So far, so good. But the strengths approach has been misapplied to mean that you should take on *only* tasks in which you are strong, not waste your time attending to your weaknesses, and in areas where you aren't strong and don't have natural talent, you or the organization should assign those tasks to other people.

That's not to say that people shouldn't attend to their strengths or that they aren't happier and more successful if they're using their strengths at work and in other aspects of their lives, but the emphasis on strengths has fundamentally discouraged people from challenging themselves to become better leaders. They can just throw up their hands and say, "Well, envisioning the future just isn't a strength of mine, so I'm not going to become very good at it." Or, "I'm not very comfortable letting people know how much I appreciate their accomplishments, so I won't bother." First, ignoring feedback about areas that you are not good at is inconsistent with a lot of research on learning (which we'll talk about later). Second, it's not very motivating to tell people to give up before they even start or the first time things don't go as well as expected. Finally, this thinking is impractical. Organizations can't bring in a new person every time someone makes a mistake or there's a new challenge that someone initially didn't have the skills and abilities to handle.

Over all the years we've been researching leadership, we've consistently found that adversity and uncertainty characterize every personal-best leadership experience (explained further in Chapter 3). Typically, they're challenges people have never faced before. Because this is true, the third fundamental of becoming an exemplary leader is *challenge yourself.* When confronting things they haven't done before, people will often have to develop new skills and overcome existing weaknesses and limitations. They make mistakes and may even feel incompetent. If people built only on strengths, they would likely not challenge themselves or their organizations. You simply can't do your best without searching for new experiences, doing things you've never done, making mistakes, and learning from them. Challenge is an important stimulus for leadership and for learning.

THE SELF-RELIANCE MYTH

No one ever made anything extraordinary happen alone. Leaders cannot possibly design breakthrough innovations, produce high-quality products, provide awesome service, attract raving fans, break sales records, ensure financial soundness and integrity, and build great places to work without the trust, teamwork, strength, and capabilities of everyone in the organization. Leadership is a team sport and not a solo performance.

Yet, there's folklore about the leader as hero who magnetizes a band of followers with courageous acts or the leader as rebel who charges headlong into the winds of resistance without regard for life or convention. There are myths about prescient visionaries with Merlin-like powers who save kingdoms, companies, industries, or nations. All this perpetuates a belief that leaders have to be self-reliant and superhuman. They have to be able to take care of themselves and get things done without the help of anyone else. They have to be independent and autonomous and never express doubts about their abilities. They can never appear in need of support or assistance—stiff upper lip, don't break a sweat, and all that balderdash.

Although there is certainly great benefit to being confident in your abilities to handle challenging situations, the best leaders know they can't do it alone. They know they need the support, engagement, and commitment of others. Isn't it intriguing to note that world-class athletes all have coaches, often more than one? These coaches are revered and celebrated—and thanked at every awards ceremony. Yet, rarely will you hear leaders even admit to having had a coach in the past, let alone one in the present, or broadcast about the training and development program they attended that helped them build their skills. They probably believe that people would consider it a weakness if they did, but just as leaders can't make extraordinary things happen all by themselves, they can't become exemplary leaders by themselves either. That's why the fourth fundamental is to *engage support* in your learning and growth.

THE IT-COMES-NATURALLY MYTH

A corollary to the myths of talent and strengths is that leadership comes naturally to those who are the best at leading. People admire those who make it seem so easy and attribute that ease to natural ability. Whether it's a performer on stage, an athlete on the court, or a leader in an organization, people assume effortless performance develops without effort. Although there may be a small percentage for whom this is true, for the vast majority this is just not so.

K. Anders Ericsson, quoted earlier, made this same point when he said, "Until most individuals recognize that sustained training and effort is a prerequisite for reaching expert levels of performance, they will continue to misattribute lesser achievement to the lack of natural gifts, and will thus fail to reach their own potential."[6]

Anders and his colleagues have found in their research that raw talent is not the only requisite to becoming a top performer. Staggeringly high IQs don't characterize the great performers, either. What actually differentiates the expert performers from the good performers is their dedication to doing something every day to improve. The truth is that the best leaders become the best because they work hard at it and put in the hours of practice. Therefore, the fifth fundamental of becoming an exemplary leader is to *practice deliberately.*

Point this observation out to would-be leaders, and they often react by saying, "I don't have the time to practice. I'm already working 10 to 12 hours a day. It's just not possible to add on another couple of hours a day to practice leading." We'd agree that you don't have any hours to add to your day. The knack is finding methods for turning your organization into a practice field and not just a playing field. There are ways you can structure your interactions with others so they become intentional practice routines. Practice is the antecedent of learning. The fundamental principle is that you have to put considerable effort into learning to lead to make leadership look effortless. No surprise that the more you practice, the easier it gets. That's why it's been said that amateurs make it look hard, and professionals make it look easy.

THE KEY MESSAGE AND ACTION

The key message in this chapter is this: Leadership potential and skills aren't talents that some people have and other people don't. They are much more broadly distributed than traditional legends suggest. You already have the capacity to lead, but some prevailing myths and assumptions about leadership get in the way of your becoming the best leader you can be. In the remainder of this book, let's confront those assumptions and learn about five fundamentals that you can apply to bust these myths, strengthen your capacity to lead, and make a difference.

SELF-COACHING ACTION

At the beginning of this chapter, we asked, "Can you, and those you work with, become better leaders than you are today?" Affirm that your answer is yes. Say aloud or silently to yourself, "I can become a better leader than I am today." Tell that to yourself daily. Make it a daily affirmation.

The next thing you should do is start a leadership journal that you can regularly use as you travel along on your leadership development journey. McGill University Management Professor Nancy Adler finds that the best way to access the insights you gain from your experiences is to reflect on them daily. "Based on research (my own and others') and many years of work with global business leaders as a consultant and international management professor," she says, "I recommend the simple act of regularly writing in a journal."[7] So, purchase a notebook or open up a document on your computer or tablet to record your daily reflections. We'll be asking you throughout this book to write down some thoughts and ideas, so make this leadership journal something you can refer to more than this once.[8]

For your first assignment in your leadership journal, write down three aspects of your leadership in which you'd like to become better. Maybe it's about further strengthening something you now do well. Maybe it's an area that isn't a strong suit but is one you feel is important to improve.

Pick one area to start. Let's say it's asking for feedback. Now write down all the ways you can think of that you could become better at asking for feedback. Don't worry at this moment whether they are practical; just brainstorm a list for yourself.

Select something from that list that you can and will do. Then, choose one colleague or friend you can trust to keep you honest in executing on it. Tell that person what you plan to do, and ask her or him to contact you daily and just inquire, "Did you do what you said you would do?"

You need to start sometime, so why not now?

CHAPTER 2

LEADERSHIP MAKES A DIFFERENCE

I t's been said that only three things happen naturally in organizations: friction, confusion, and underperformance; everything else requires leadership.[1]

Reflect for a moment on your own experience, and you can certainly appreciate why "everything else requires leadership." You know firsthand that leadership makes a difference because you've worked with some leaders who've been able to get you to give your very best, and often even a bit more, and you've worked with other people for whom you've done only what is asked of you and not much more.

We've asked thousands of people to think about the worst leader and the best leader they've ever worked with. We then posed the following question: What percentage of your talents (skills and ability plus time and energy) would you say each of these leaders brought out? We then asked them to give us a percentage from 1 to 100.

When people think about their experience with their *worst* leader, the percentage of talent used typically ranges between 2 and 40 percent, with an average of 31 percent. People report that in their experience with their worst leader, they used less than a third of their available talents. Many continued to work hard, but few put all that they were capable of delivering into their work. Exit interviews reveal a similar phenomenon—people aren't quitting their company as much as they are quitting the relationship with their manager. A Gallup survey shows that 50 percent of people at some point in their careers have left their job to get away from their manager.[2]

This dismal situation is in sharp contrast with what people report when they think about their experience with their best leader. These leaders bring out a minimum of 40 percent of their talent, and note that this *bottom* was the top of the range for the *worst* leaders. In fact, many claim that their best leaders actually got more than 100 percent of their talent! You know that it's mathematically impossible to get more than 100 percent of an individual's talent, and yet people shake their heads and say, "No, they really did get me to do more than I thought I was capable of doing or that it was possible to do." The average percentage of talent people's best leaders elicited is a whopping 95 percent.

There's clearly a difference between people's worst and best leaders. As illustrated in Figure 2.1, the best leaders bring out more than three times the amount of talent, energy, and motivation from their people compared with their counterparts at the other end of the spectrum.

Amelia Klawon, account manager at Moves the Needle, added further insight into these numbers when she remarked how a leader's behavior affects people's confidence in their abilities in their current position and even in future positions. She explained: "I had some people who micromanaged what I did and were quick to criticize and slow to give praise. I started to become more cautious and less confident in my ability to perform in that position and subsequent positions until

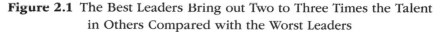

Figure 2.1 The Best Leaders Bring out Two to Three Times the Talent in Others Compared with the Worst Leaders

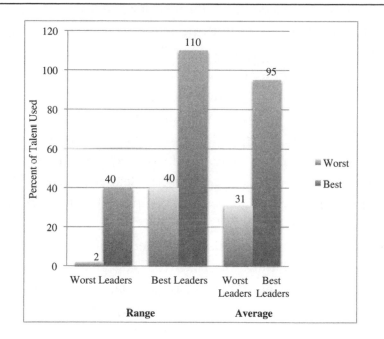

I worked for someone who believed in me, pushed me, and gave me room to rise to the challenge and lead others. Bad leadership can be very harmful and cause long-term damage to one's confidence and performance that is not easy or quick to repair."

The data confirm that leadership makes a difference. That difference can be negative or positive, but it does make a difference. Leadership has an impact on people's commitment, their desire to stay or leave, their willingness to put forth more discretionary effort, and their inclination to take personal initiative and responsibility. Bad leaders have a dampening effect on these things, and exemplary leaders have just the opposite effect. What sort of difference do you want to achieve through your leadership? The choice is yours.

LEADERSHIP AND ENGAGEMENT LEVELS

There are many reports these days about employee engagement and the impact it has on both personal well-being and organizational productivity. Our studies find that how one's leader behaves explains more than any other variable about why people feel engaged or not in their workplace.[3] Multiple regression analyses, using data from more than 650,000 direct reports, reveal that nearly 37 percent of the variance in levels of employee engagement is accounted for by how frequently they see the individual they report to engaging in leadership behaviors—specifically The Five Practices of Exemplary Leadership (which we introduce in Chapter 3).[4]

Could engagement levels be better explained by various individual and organizational factors? The answer is no. Such potentially significant and interesting variables as people's age, educational level, gender, functional area, hierarchical level, industry, length of time with the company, size of the organization, or nationality together account for no more than one-tenth of one percent (0.1 percent) in the variation around individuals' levels of engagement. Table 2.1 compares the impact of demographics versus leadership on engagement levels around the world. Clearly, how you behave as a leader matters the most to others.

There's abundant evidence that how leaders behave makes a difference across a variety of settings. For example, what effect do the leadership behaviors of teachers have on classroom effectiveness and student achievement? Researchers find that "students have an overwhelmingly strong positive reaction to teachers who demonstrate leadership in the classroom," and it plays a major role in the reaction, behavior, and learning of students.[5] An investigation into the leadership skills of all-star baseball players concluded that it doesn't matter if you are "part of a team of lawyers sitting in luxury office chairs in a

Table 2.1 Percentage of Engagement Explained by Leadership Practices and Demographics across Countries

Country	Leadership	Demographics
Australia	37.0%	0.3%
Brazil	34.0%	0.5%
Canada	34.0%	0.5%
China	54.4%	0.3%
Egypt	41.9%	3.8%
France	34.1%	1.9%
Germany	39.3%	0.2%
India	45.2%	0.5%
Indonesia	42.6%	1.0%
Ireland	46.9%	1.3%
Israel	39.3%	1.5%
Italy	33.4%	2.1%
Japan	42.9%	1.3%
New Zealand	36.5%	0.7%
Philippines	29.9%	1.0%
Russia	49.4%	0.3%
Saudi Arabia	47.4%	0.4%
Singapore	39.8%	0.9%
South Africa	36.9%	1.0%
South Korea	54.7%	0.8%
United Kingdom	33.9%	0.4%
United States	36.0%	0.1%

conference room or part of a team of baseball players sitting on pine benches in a locker room. It matters not if the respondent is a lawyer or a mail clerk; an all-star center field or a bat boy. . . . What matters is how they behave."[6] Caroline Wang, with more than 30 years of working experience in the United States and across Asia Pacific, and serving on the board of directors for three multinational companies in China, explained, "When it comes to leadership it is not about the leader's personality; it is all about how that individual behaves as a leader."

It certainly makes sense that how leaders behave explains how engaged their direct reports are in the workplace, but what you might not expect is that the leaders' own behavior also explains how they feel about the workplace. Using the same measurements that we used with direct reports, we asked leaders to indicate their levels of workplace engagement. Those more frequently demonstrating exemplary leader behaviors felt significantly more engaged and positive about their workplace than those leaders who reported demonstrating leadership less frequently. We found a similar result when we studied volunteers with a national youth sports organization. The more they reported engaging in leadership, the more attachment and pride they felt about the organization and their experience with it.[7] This should not be surprising. The more you invest in making something special happen for others, the more attachment you feel to what you are doing and the organization you are involved with.

When people reflect on their experiences, it becomes clear that the way leaders behave has an impact on both themselves and others around them. Leadership makes a significant and meaningful difference in the willingness of people to put forth great discretionary effort and, in turn, perform beyond expectations. When this happens, you benefit and everyone else does, too.

LEADERS ARE DIFFERENT WHILE LEADERSHIP IS THE SAME

There is no single mold or distinct personality profile for leadership. Leaders come in all types, shapes, sizes, and colors. There is not one look or style. You are unique, and you don't have to be anyone else but who you are.

You'll find leaders in public and private organizations, from large to small companies, from new to mature industries, from low-tech to high-tech, from cities, communities, and neighborhoods to synagogues, mosques, churches, temples, and athletic teams. There are even pockets of leaders in low-performing and underperforming organizations.

What differentiates leaders from nonleaders is not so much outside the person (the exterior) as it is the interior. Leadership is not a position or place in an organization. It's not confined to a particular job description. Underscoring this point is an experience we had after introducing a senior corporate executive to the students in one of our classes. While thanking us for the introduction, he commented, "That is my title and position in this organization, but it doesn't tell you who I am." He then went on to explain where he grew up, his family, educational experiences, and how all those things influenced him. And then he added, "Who I am is not simply what I do." Similarly, leadership is not simply what *you* do.

Every leader is different because of who he or she is. And yet, every leader is similar because there are definable skills, abilities, and mindsets that differentiate leaders from nonleaders. You have to know who you are—that's essential—and you need to know what exemplary leaders do and how they think to become the best leader you can be.

The point we want to make is that leadership actions and behaviors make a difference across a wide variety of settings, circumstances, and environments. The key empirical takeaway from our research is that effective leaders demonstrate exemplary leader behaviors more frequently than their less effective colleagues do. Although people can differ in how they demonstrate each behavior, leaders must express them more frequently to increase the engagement and performance of their constituents.

For example, consider the impact of leadership behavior on healthcare leaders working for the same organization in Ethiopia, India, Pakistan, and the Philippines. Empirical analyses both across and within each country were conducted, from self and constituent perspectives. Although how often leaders used The Five Practices of Exemplary Leadership varied across countries, within the countries their impact on constituents was the same. Within each country, the more frequently those leaders used the leadership practices, the more effective constituents viewed them, and the more favorable both their own and constituents' levels of engagement were.[8]

Furthermore, while some studies suggest that people from different cultures expect different behaviors from their leaders, there is growing evidence of a homogenizing effect from globalization. Think about it this way: If organizational expectations are converging on a global standard, then people around the world should have similar expectations of their leaders; the same leader behaviors should increase people's satisfaction levels with their leader, regardless of the individual's cultural background.[9]

We tested this assertion with representatives from all the world's cultural zones. The results were consistent with the hypothesis. Using The Five Practices of Exemplary Leadership as predictors of people's satisfaction with their leader, we found similar results across the world. In nearly 100 percent of the cases, the effect of a given leadership behavior on constituent satisfaction was comparable, regardless of that person's cultural background. People around the world have similar expectations about how leaders should behave and therefore have similar evaluations of what makes their leaders effective. Although you might expect differences between groups—for example, by nationality, function, industry, ethnicity, age, and so on—you won't find differences within groups when it comes to assessing leadership effectiveness.

Leaders can differ in lots of personal ways, but exemplary leaders universally engage in very similar practices. You are a unique person, but there are common leadership practices that bring out the best in others. We'll take a brief look at those in the next chapter.

THE KEY MESSAGE AND ACTION

The key message of this chapter is this: Leadership makes a significant difference in levels of engagement and commitment. Developing your leadership capabilities will help you improve the way you and others feel about your workplace and promote more productive organizations. Learning to be a better leader also enhances your feelings of self-worth and meaningfulness. Although circumstances and contexts vary, the process of leadership remains relatively constant.

SELF-COACHING ACTION

Take a few moments to reflect upon the following questions and make some notes in your leadership journal:

- What difference do I want to make?
- Are my actions making the difference I want to make?
- Do my actions help bring out the best in myself and others?

How aligned are your answers with your aspirations? What does your answer mean for you? What do you need to be doing differently?

CHAPTER 3

YOU ARE ALREADY LEADING—JUST NOT FREQUENTLY ENOUGH

W e've collected Personal-Best Leadership Experiences from thousands of people around the world. A personal best experience is an event (or series of events) that people believe is their individual standard of excellence. It is their "record-setting performance," so to speak: the time when they did their very best. It is something people use to measure themselves by: the time they look upon as their peak or highest-performing experience.

The experience does not need to be restricted to a time when someone was an appointed or selected leader. It can be either a time when they emerged as the informal leader or a time when they were the official leader, manager, supervisor, or captain. It can be in any functional area, in a service or manufacturing organization, in a public or private institution, in a staff or line position. It can be the start-up of a new business, a new product or service development program, quality or productivity improvement project, turnaround, crisis, and so on.

The experience does not need to be in one's current organization. It can be in a past work experience, or even a family or volunteer setting. It can be in a club, professional organization, school, team, congregation, or any other setting. It can any time when the person feels that they performed at his or her best as a leader.

After asking thousands of people to do this, from all kinds of nationalities, industries and functions, hierarchical levels, ages, genders, and the like, what we discovered has significant implications for developing leaders and leadership. The data told us empirically that:

1. *Everyone* has a leadership story to tell.
2. The leadership actions and behaviors across these cases are much more similar than different.

Obviously, the individuals responding to the Personal-Best Leadership Experience questionnaire are different from one another along myriad factors and characteristics, and over the years, the context or circumstances of these experiences have varied. Even so, when people share with one another their leadership experiences, they have little difficulty identifying situations in which they led and the actions they took to make extraordinary things happen. Additionally, they can easily identify common behaviors demonstrated across the leadership stories they hear. The bottom-line conclusions from their own discussions, and in their words, are that "everyone is capable of leadership" and "leadership is not so esoteric or ephemeral that it cannot be observed and described."

This is precisely what Gowri Narayanaswami, worldwide channels program manager at Cisco Systems, told us. She had assumed that leaders had certain traits and qualities, and these were not traits she identified with herself. She thought, like many people, that there were natural leaders who were born to lead and that leadership is associated with occupation and position. Yet when she reflected on her personal-best leadership experience, she realized, much to her initial surprise, that she herself "had engaged in those same leadership behaviors and demonstrated ability as a leader." Alternatively, consider what Harmail Chatha, Groupon's global data center operations director, realized after listening to his colleagues share their personal-best leadership experiences: "Leadership is all around us. It comes in all manner of shapes and sizes, and applies to each one of us."

What's your personal-best leadership story, and what do you already know firsthand about leadership from your experience? Think about this for a moment, and keep it in the back of your mind as you read the remainder of this chapter.

THE FIVE PRACTICES OF EXEMPLARY LEADERSHIP®

From our analysis of thousands of personal-best leadership case studies and interviews, we've discovered that ordinary people who guide others along pioneering journeys follow rather similar paths. Though each experience was unique in expression, every case followed remarkably parallel patterns of action. We've grouped these common practices into a leadership framework we call The Five Practices of Exemplary Leadership.[1] The Five Practices are not the private property of the people we studied or of a few select shining stars. Leadership is not about personality; it's about behavior. The Five Practices are not the accident of a unique moment in history. They have stood the tests of time and place. Moreover, hundreds of scholars have used this framework in their own studies of leadership, investigating the central role leadership plays in personal well-being and organizational productivity and effectiveness.[2]

These leadership practices are available to you and others who want to become the best leaders they can be.[3] These are The Five Practices along with the two key essential leadership commitments connected with each one:

Model the Way
- Clarify values by finding your voice and affirming shared values
- Set the example by aligning actions with shared values

Inspire a Shared Vision
- Envision the future by imagining exciting and ennobling possibilities
- Enlist others in a common vision by appealing to shared aspirations

Challenge the Process
- Search for opportunities by seizing the initiative and by looking outward for innovative ways to improve
- Experiment and take risks by constantly generating small wins and learning from experience

Enable Others to Act
- Foster collaboration by building trust and facilitating relationships
- Strengthen others by increasing self-determination and developing competence

Encourage the Heart
- Recognize contributions by showing appreciation for individual excellence
- Celebrate the values and victories by creating a spirit of community

This framework, as we reported in Chapter 2, demonstrates a remarkable ability, around the world, to illuminate why people feel positively engaged in their workplaces. No other single variable, in fact, explains more than leadership does when it comes to understanding what makes organizations work most effectively.

LEADERSHIP IS WITHIN EVERYONE'S CAPABILITIES

Once we had derived this model from the thousands of case studies, we developed the Leadership Practices Inventory (LPI) as a way to measure the practices.[4] The LPI provides feedback on how often individuals are currently engaging in the leadership behaviors and actions that are associated with leaders being at their personal best. The LPI comprises 30 leadership behaviors (six for each one of The Five Practices). For example:

1. I set a personal example of what I expect of others. (Model)
2. I describe a compelling image of what our future could look like. (Inspire)
3. I search outside the formal boundaries of my organization for innovative ways to improve what we do. (Challenge)
4. I support the decisions people make on their own. (Enable)
5. I find ways to celebrate accomplishments. (Encourage)

Each behavior is assessed on a 10-point frequency scale from one, indicating "almost never," to 10, indicating "almost always" engage in the behavior described. More than 2.5 million people globally have completed the current edition of the LPI, representing a robust sample of nationalities, personalities, disciplines, and organizations. The LPI provides a 360-degree look—from the leader's own perspective, as well as the vantage point of his or her managers, colleagues, direct reports, and others—at the extent to which the actions identified as key leadership behaviors are being used.

In more than 30 years of collecting data using the LPI, practically *no one* who completed the instrument has scored a zero across all five leadership practices—that is, to be precise, less than 0.00044 percent gave themselves a response score of "almost never" engaging in all 30 of the leadership behaviors on the instrument. In a more positive light, approximately 99.99956 percent of all leaders who have taken the LPI report frequency scores above zero (that is, above "almost never"). The percentage above "almost never" is even higher from all the people assessing these leaders: 99.99987 percent. From the perspective of their managers, 99.9999 percent report frequency scores for their direct reports on The Five Practices greater than zero. From coworkers and peers, 99.99987 percent of the scores they give their colleagues are above zero. Furthermore, in 99.99985 percent of the cases, direct reports indicate that their leaders engage in The Five Practices more than "almost never."

Do the math and look around. You'll find that the chance of finding someone with a score of zero in a 100-person organization is zero. In a 1,000-person organization, the probability of finding someone with a score of zero is zero. In a 10,000-person organization, the chance of finding someone with a score of zero is still nearly zero.

These results underscore the earlier assertion that everyone is capable of engaging in the leadership behaviors identified as essential to achieving record-setting standards of excellence. The inescapable fact is *not* that people aren't leading (or capable of leadership) but that people are *not leading frequently enough*! How about you? Are you leading frequently enough?

LEADERSHIP FREQUENCY IS RELATED TO EFFECTIVENESS AND PRODUCTIVITY

Hundreds of studies by independent researchers have found that the extent to which people engage in these five leadership practices are consistently associated with important aspects of managerial and organizational effectiveness, such as work group performance, team cohesiveness, commitment, satisfaction, motivation, and productivity.[5] Studies show that the frequency to which these leadership behaviors are used relates positively with, for example, employee retention,[6] classroom achievement,[7] worksite safety,[8] congregational growth,[9] emotional intelligence,[10] resilience,[11] performance of family businesses,[12] and quality of patient care.[13]

How frequently people report that their leaders engage in The Five Practices of Exemplary Leadership relates directly to their level of engagement (as shown in the previous chapter). In addition, this relationship is unaffected by characteristics of the respondents. In other words, demographic factors about direct reports do not illuminate why they are or are not engaged in the workplace, but knowing how they see their leader behaving provides a substantial explanation for their levels of engagement.

In completing the LPI, respondents also evaluate the overall effectiveness of their leader. The direct reports who strongly agree their leader is effective can then be compared with direct reports whose evaluations are less favorable in terms of how frequently each group observes the leaders using The Five Practices. This analysis shows (see Table 3.1) that the leaders who are reported as most effective (strong) by their direct reports are also seen as engaging significantly ($p < .001$) more often in The Five Practices than leaders viewed as less effective (low/moderate).

Table 3.1 Leader Effectiveness Rating by Direct Reports and Use of
The Five Practices of Exemplary Leadership

Leader Effectiveness	*Leadership Practices*				
	Model	Inspire	Challenge	Enable	Encourage
Low/Moderate	42.62	40.36	40.81	46.20	41.62
Strong	53.50	51.76	51.58	55.58	53.16

The truth is that you are already leading. Everyone we have ever studied is leading to some extent. This may not be the popular opinion, but it's a fact. Leadership is much more available to you than possibly you or others may think. Too often leadership is associated with position—with kings and queens, chief executive officers (CEOs) and presidents, and charismatic politicians and revolutionary movement figures. Some of these people are certainly providing leadership, but they are not the only ones.

Those people the media typically associate with leadership are not anywhere near the top of the list when it comes to admired leader role models. Most leadership role models, according to our research findings, are closer to home. Whether you are a high school student or workplace professional, more than three-quarters of the leadership role models whom people select are family members, a teacher or coach, or an immediate manager at work.[14] These are not just the people you know but also the folks who know you.

However, no one is going to follow you for very long if you aren't willing to follow yourself, and that's the idea explored in the next chapter.

THE KEY MESSAGE AND ACTION

The key message of this chapter is this: Everyone has a story to tell about the time he or she was leading and making a difference. In addition, there is a common set of leadership practices—behaviors and actions—associated with leadership that is within the capacity of everyone to use. The challenge is how to increase the frequency with which you engage in these leadership practices, learning about what they mean and becoming more comfortable and confident in their use.

SELF-COACHING ACTION

Put aside some time to reflect on your own Personal-Best Leadership Experience. Here are some ideas to guide your reflection and analysis:

1. Describe the situation. Who was involved, and what was your role?
2. Why did you take on this initiative, how did you experiment and challenge existing ways of doing things, and how did you deal with risks?
3. As you looked forward to the time when the project would be completed, what did you dream about, and how did you build a sense of enthusiasm and excitement for the endeavor and reflect the hopes and dreams of other people on the team?
4. How did you involve others in planning and decision making, foster cooperation, build trust, and enhance the competence and confidence of your colleagues?
5. What were the values that you held yourself and others accountable to, and how did you lead by example and keep yourself focused and not sidetracked?
6. How did you recognize individual contributions, celebrate team accomplishments, create a spirit of camaraderie, and generate genuine appreciation?

After thinking through your experience and these questions, write down in your leadership journal the five to seven key leadership actions you took that enabled this to be a personal-best leadership experience. What would you say you learned from this leadership experience? What would you teach someone else based upon your own personal-best leadership experience?

PART II

FUNDAMENTAL ONE: BELIEVE YOU CAN

Believing that you can lead is essential to developing your leadership skills and abilities. If you don't believe this, it's unlikely that you will make any effort at all, let alone a sustained effort to become a better leader over time. No one can put leadership into you. You have to bring it out of yourself.

The best leaders are the best learners. They have a growth mindset. They believe that they are capable of learning and developing throughout their lives. Continuous learning is a way of life for exemplary leaders, so you are never done learning and never done getting better. You can reflect, read, watch others, get a coach, attend some training, or just try out a new skill or technique. Whatever your learning style is, engage in it every day.

Authentic leadership flows from the inside out. You have to liberate that capacity you already have, and that begins by taking an inner journey to discover who you are. You already have it in you to lead. Don't let anyone tell you that you don't make a difference.

In the next three chapters we take a look at these key themes on becoming an exemplary leader:

- You have to believe in yourself.
- Learning is the master skill.
- Leadership emerges from within.

CHAPTER 4

YOU HAVE TO BELIEVE IN YOURSELF

U p to this point in this book, we've made three bold assertions, all supported by research evidence. Everyone, including you, is born with the capacity to lead. Leaders have an enormous impact on the engagement and performance of their constituents. And, you are already leading, just not frequently enough.

Now let's do a reality check. Do you believe these statements? Do you believe deep down that you are capable of becoming a better leader tomorrow than you are today? Alternatively, do you believe that there's not a whole lot you can do to improve? Either you have it, or you don't? These are not trivial questions. They get to the heart of the matter. They get to the very belief that you have about yourself.

Underscoring this same point is an old Native American parable. It conveys the message that who you become is strongly influenced by the image you have of yourself. Those assumptions strongly influence the actions that you take. It goes like this:

One evening, an old Cherokee Indian told his grandson
about a battle that goes on inside people. He said, "My

son, the battle is between two wolves inside us all. One is Evil. It is anger, envy, jealousy, sorrow, regret, greed, arrogance, self-pity, guilt, resentment, inferiority, lies, false pride, superiority, and ego. The other is Good. It is joy, peace, love, hope, serenity, humility, kindness, benevolence, empathy, generosity, truth, compassion, and faith."

The grandson thought about it for a minute and then asked his grandfather, "Which wolf wins?"

The grandfather replied, "The one you feed."

The Buddha echoed pretty much the same sentiment back in the fifth century BC: "All that we are is the result of what we have thought. The mind is everything. What we think, we become."[1]

Learning to lead has very similar roots. It all starts with what you think of yourself and the assumptions you feed.

Learning to lead is about discovering what *you* value, what inspires *you*, what challenges *you*, what gives *you* energy, and what encourages *you*. When you discover these things about yourself, you'll also know more about what it takes to lead those qualities out of others. The very best education—whether it's in school or the workplace—is never about thrusting information or skills into people. In the end that just won't work. The best education is about bringing out, sometimes even liberating, what is already there. It's about releasing the potential that exists inside the learner. It's about making choices about which wolf to feed.

Sure, every leader has to learn the fundamentals and the discipline, and there are periods during which you're trying out many things you know nothing about and you have no idea what will work and what won't. There are times when you copy others and absorb a lot of information from the outside. These are necessary stages in your development as a leader. The point is that you can't begin to do any of these things until you *truly decide that inside of you is a person who can make a difference and provide leadership.*

TAKE THE MIRROR TEST

When we were in New Orleans a couple of years ago for the sixth annual "The Leadership Challenge Forum," we happened separately upon an art gallery. In the gallery, there was a Jim Tweedy print of a rather plump cat sitting on a stool at an artist's easel painting a self-portrait.[2] With a brush grasped in one paw and the side of the canvas in another, the cat was looking into the mirror and seeing his reflection staring back at him. On the easel, however, was the painting not of a plump cat but of a very fierce tiger. We later discovered that we both bought copies because the print made us laugh aloud at the irony in the drawing.

Some who see this painting comment that the cat is delusional. He's just kidding himself. Clearly, the cat's just a cat and not a tiger. But others view this as an expression of inner potential. They know there's more there than meets the eye. What you see on the outside isn't necessarily what's on the inside. Looks, as the saying goes, can be deceiving.

Both interpretations are possible. What's important is how you see it. When you look in your own mirror, do you see a leader? Do you see someone who on the inside has the potential to become a leader—or be an even better one than you are today—or do you see someone not capable of leading or making any improvements? What do you *believe* about yourself? These are really important questions. What are your answers?

Jane Blake, a state government administrator, shifted her entire self-concept once she started believing that she could be a leader.[3] She told us that she'd been working in state government for about 20 years, that she had two bachelor's degrees, and that she never wanted to appear more than what she was—"a mother, grandmother, and coal miner's daughter." At the time, she was enrolled in a master's degree program in leadership, and she sometimes struggled with the coursework and felt intimidated by classmates who were military leaders, company supervisors, and government managers. However, Jane explained that reading about leadership in one of our books "opened my eyes that maybe someone like me does have the possibility of being a leader." That's precisely the point. That's what can happen when you reflect on your life story up to this present moment and appreciate that you, too, have the possibility of being a leader—or, if you are already leading, that you can become an even better leader than you are today.

Over a couple of decades, Jane had created a narrative for her life. She'd told herself a story about who she was and what she was capable of becoming based on being a mother, grandmother, and coal miner's daughter. Like Jane, all people create a narrative about their lives based on their experiences, what others have told them, and what they read and hear in school, in the media, or over dinner with friends. These narratives help you make sense of your life. They help you explain what's happening and why you are where you are and who you are.

But sometimes they become what Michael Hyatt, publishing executive and author, describes as limiting beliefs. These beliefs, Michael says, are invisible barriers. They're not physical barriers that are out there, such as electric fences, but instead, they're barriers people erect in their minds that nonetheless stop them from going beyond the invisible limits. "It's just a way of thinking. We've been trained on it over and over again and it becomes a limiting belief, something that holds us back from having the kind of relationship we want, the kind of health we want, the kind of career we want, the kind of financial success we want."[4] As Jane learned from her own experience, it wasn't something "out there" that held her back.

It was a limiting narrative that, once she realized it, she could change.

We heard something very similar from Dan Wong, product manager at computer software company [24]7. Upon reflecting on what he was learning from his and others' Personal-Best Leadership Experiences, Dan said, "You point out a very vital attribute of leaders that I was not aware of: Leaders believe in their abilities to make a difference. The very first step to become a better leader is to acknowledge that I can improve my leadership skills and remind myself that I can make a difference. All I need is a positive mindset to look for opportunities and a willingness to take initiative."

Jane and Dan both understand that before you can learn to lead, you have to *believe* you can. This is no trivial matter. No one can make you into a leader. You have to do that all by yourself. Believing in your capabilities to execute on a task is vital in taking the first step to attempt it. If you don't believe you can lead, then you won't even try. As Adlai Stevenson, former governor of Illinois and the fifth U.S. ambassador to the United Nations, once humorously put it, "It's hard to lead a cavalry charge if you think you look funny on a horse."

DON'T LET ANYONE TELL YOU THAT YOU CAN'T LEAD

If you don't believe in yourself and in your ideas, then it's difficult to imagine that anyone else would pay attention to you. Leadership has to start with you. Just like Dorothy in *The Wizard of Oz*, you can't look for someone behind the curtain to solve your problems. The very first voice of doubt is often the one inside of you, and unless you believe in yourself and can deal with that self-doubt, it is unlikely that you'll speak out, stand up, or step forward.

Melissa Poe Hood, as a fourth grader in Nashville, Tennessee, became concerned about the environment, and decided to do something about it. She started a club in 1989 called Kids F.A.C.E. (Kids For A Clean Environment), which is today the world's largest youth environmental organization, with more than 300,000 individual members in 2,000 club chapters located in 15 countries. Looking back on that experience two decades later, Melissa noted that: "Change does not begin with someone else. Change begins in your own backyard, no matter your age or your size. I had no idea that one simple action could change my life so much. Most journeys start this way, with simple motivation and a choice to do something or not. You never know where one step will take you, and you never know where the next one will lead. The difference with being a leader is that you take the step; you take the journey. The greatest obstacle you will ever encounter is yourself."

Just as Melissa realized, you have to believe in yourself. You have to trust yourself. You have to have confidence in yourself. You have to be convinced deep down that you have as much capacity to lead as anyone else you know. You won't always be right, but you'll become an active learner and more proficient in the process.

But it's not just what you tell yourself that can keep you from exercising leadership. All too often, what others tell you influences you to give up. In fact, one of the most adverse consequences of the talent myth is that, if interpreted rigidly, it inhibits people from attempting to become leaders. Told that leadership is limited to only a few with the special talent for leading, people can conclude that they can't learn it, and so they don't attempt it—or they give up once they find that it's not easy, or they blame it on the lack of talent. Don't let yourself become one of those people who doesn't try. Don't let anyone tell you that you can't lead.

In a series of classic experiments, professors Albert Bandura and Robert Wood documented that self-efficacy—defined as an individual's belief in his or her capacity to produce specific actions—affects people's performance.[5] One group of managers was told that decision making was a skill developed through practice: The more one worked at it, the more capable one became. Another group of managers was told that decision making reflected their basic intellectual aptitude—the higher their underlying cognitive capacities, the better their decision-making ability. Working with a simulated organization, both groups of managers dealt with a series of production orders requiring various staffing decisions and establishing different performance targets.

Managers who believed that decision making was a skill that could be acquired set challenging goals for themselves—even in the face of difficult performance standards—used good problem-solving strategies, and fostered organizational productivity. Their counterparts, who didn't believe they had the necessary decision-making ability, lost confidence in themselves as they encountered difficulties. Over multiple trials, they lowered their aspirations for the organization, their problem solving deteriorated, and organizational productivity declined.[6]

Another important finding from these studies was that the managers who lost confidence in their own judgments dealt with this by finding fault with others. They were quite uncharitable about their employees, regarding them as not capable of being motivated and unworthy of much supervisory effort. If given the option, the managers reported that they would have fired many of these employees.

In another related experiment, one group of managers was told that organizations and people are easily changeable, and another group was told that "work habits of employees are not that easily changeable, even by good guidance. Small changes do not necessarily improve overall outcomes." Those managers with the belief that they could influence organizational outcomes by their actions maintained a higher level of performance over time than those who felt they could do little to change things. The latter group lost faith in their capabilities, and as their aspirations declined so did organizational performance levels.[7]

These studies and many others demonstrate why it is essential that you don't let people tell you that you can't lead—or if they do, that you don't believe them. The subjects in these various studies were *randomly* assigned to the different groups. The difference in their performance was not because one group was inherently better than the other group at decision making. It was because they were *told* that they had the ability or they didn't. If you happen to fall in the unfortunate group who's told that you can't lead, there's a chance that you'll believe it, and then your performance, and the performance of your group, will decline. Moreover, you're also likely to pass those beliefs on to others.

Of course, everyone has limitations as well as strengths. And learning to lead isn't necessarily easy. In fact, it's hard work but definitely doable. What we are saying is that you shouldn't give in to your limitations or accept them as permanent. When you doubt yourself, confront this feeling, and then do something to acquire the skills needed to handle a similar encounter in the future. That's the essence of learning!

Your default belief needs to be that you can learn to lead. That's the primary belief that will enable you to become a better leader than you are right now.

THE KEY MESSAGE AND ACTION

The key message of this chapter is this: Believing that you can lead is absolutely essential to developing your leadership skills and abilities. It's this belief that provides you the commitment and sustained effort needed to become a better leader over time. No one can put leadership into you. You have to bring it out of yourself. That process begins when you believe that you can.

SELF-COACHING ACTION

Ask experienced elite athletes what the difference is between the top performers and the average performers, and they're most likely to tell you that the difference is how athletes play the mental game. In leadership, as in sports, there's a mental side to the endeavor. You saw in your Personal-Best Leadership Experience that you've done it before. You can do it again . . . and again, and again. You have to trust that you can do that.

So here's what you need to do. Every morning as you prepare for your day, tell yourself, "Who I am, what I do, and how I do it make a difference." And then ask yourself, "Today, what will I do that matters?" Whatever it is, make sure you tell that person in the mirror that you *believe* you can make a positive difference in the world. Go one step further: Write your answer to this question down, and have it with you on your mobile phone or at your desk as a reminder available throughout your day.

CHAPTER 5

LEARNING IS THE MASTER SKILL

We have a question for you. Have you ever learned a new game or a new sport?

Undoubtedly, your answer is yes. We get that response every time we ask the question in our classes or leadership development programs. Invariably every hand in the room goes up.

We then ask, "And how many of you got it perfect the first day you played it?" People chuckle. No hands go up. No one ever gets it right the first time.

There was one occasion, however, when Urban Hilger, Jr. raised his hand and said that on the very first day he went skiing he got it perfect. Naturally we were surprised and curious, so we asked Urban to tell us about the experience. Here's what he said:

> It was the first day of skiing classes. I skied all day long, and I didn't fall down once. I was so elated. I felt so good. So I skied up to the instructor, and I told him of my great day. You know what the ski instructor said? He told me, "Personally, Urban, I think you had a lousy day."

> I was stunned. "What do you mean lousy day? I thought the objective was to stand up on these boards, not fall down."
>
> The ski instructor looked me straight in the eyes and replied, "Urban, if you're not falling, you're not learning."

Urban's ski instructor understood that if you can stand up on your skis all day long the first time out, you're only doing what you already know how to do and not pushing yourself to try anything new and difficult. By definition learning is about something you don't already know. Those who do what they already know how to do may have lots of experience, but after a while they don't get any better because they aren't learning anything new. Research has shown that teachers, for example, improve during their first five years in the field, as measured by student learning, according to University of Virginia psychology professor Daniel Willingham. He goes on to report, however, that after five years their performance curve goes flat, and a teacher with 20 years of experience, on average, is no better or worse than a teacher with 10. Says Dan, "It appears that most teachers work on their teaching until it is above some threshold and they are satisfied with their proficiency."[1] The same might be said about many leaders.

So ask yourself: Are you pushing yourself to learn something new when it comes to leadership every day? Or, are you just doing what you already know how to do? Are you stretching yourself to go beyond your comfort zone—beyond what you do well enough—and engaging in activities that test you and build new skills? Are you learning?

THE BEST LEADERS ARE THE BEST LEARNERS

Over the years we've conducted a series of empirical studies to find out whether leaders learned differently than others; was there something special or unique about their learning styles or aptitudes?[2] We wanted to know whether the way leaders were learning played a role in how effective they were at leading. Although there are many different ways to learn—for example, by taking action (e.g., preferring to learn by trial and error); by thinking (e.g., reading articles or books or going online to gain knowledge and background); by feeling (e.g., confronting themselves on what areas they are worrying about); and by accessing others (e.g., bouncing hopes and fears off someone they trust)—people can be differentiated by the range and depth of learning tactics they use when facing a new or unfamiliar experience.

The results from these studies have been most intriguing. First, we found that you could learn leadership in a variety of ways. Second, certain learning styles contribute to more effectiveness in some leadership practices than others do, but there is no one best style for learning everything there is to know about leadership. The style was not what led to achievement.

What turned out to be most important was the *extent* to which individuals engaged in whatever learning style worked for them. Those leaders who were more engaged in each of their preferred learning styles, regardless of what their styles were, also more frequently engaged in The Five Practices of Exemplary Leadership. Learning to lead is not dependent on any particular learning style.

It doesn't matter how you learn. What matters is that you *do more of* whatever learning tactic works best for you. Clearly linked to becoming a better leader is becoming a better learner. The best leaders are the best learners.

This shouldn't be news to anyone. It just makes sense that those people who push themselves to learn will do better than those who only dabble in it. Attending one three-day workshop, reading one best-selling book, reflecting only on one critical incident, or participating in one simulation doesn't produce great leaders. Nor does it produce great musicians, physicians, engineers, teachers, accountants, computer scientists, or writers. To become the best at anything, you have to learn continuously.

These findings also raise an extremely interesting and mostly unexplored question: Which comes first, learning or leading? Whenever we pursue this question with our clients their hunches are the same as ours. Learning comes first. When people are predisposed to be curious and *want to* learn something new—as compared with those who aren't inclined to view learning as an important part of their daily lives—they are much more likely to reflect, read, experiment with a new behavior, attend a course, get a coach, or initiate some other mode of learning. They are also less likely to see feedback as a threat and more likely to see mistakes and failures as opportunities for growth and development.

For example, at the end of his first full year as a management consultant, former Harvard business faculty member David Maister, at the age of 39, decided to take stock, and he asked himself what assets he had as a professional consultant. This in-depth internal audit was a turning point in his career. He had, first, his knowledge and skill, and, second, he had his client relationships. David began to comprehend that these were interdependent. If he relied only upon what he already knew, then he would acquire clients who needed what he knew at that time. That, he surmised, was a finite number. Worse yet, his existing clients had already been served by what he already knew, so they were not likely to hire him again unless he learned more. Then it hit him. He hadn't learned anything new in his first year on his own, and unless he actively worked at it, his career prospects would inevitably decline.[3]

David's story gives testimony to the fact that if you want to be hired—or if you want to be a leader—you have to look within yourself to improve and move on. As you conduct your own value audit, what do you see as your unique talents? What are your strengths? What are your weaknesses? What kind of feedback are you getting about how you affect others? What are the themes in this feedback? What is it telling you about yourself? Where are you succeeding? Where are you failing? What value are you providing that no one else can? Your answers to questions like these will both inform and guide you about areas that you need to explore and learn more about.

Learning is the master skill. When you fully engage in learning—when you throw yourself wholeheartedly into experimenting, reflecting, reading, or getting coaching—you're going to experience improvement. Perhaps even greatness. Less is not more when it comes to learning. More is more. When it comes to getting great at leading or anything for that matter, you have to keep on learning.

YES, YOU CAN LEARN TO LEAD

Leadership has often been referred to as a set of traits, styles, personality types, or strengths. All of these perspectives have some value in understanding the topic, but at its most fundamental level leadership is best understood as an observable pattern of actions and behaviors. It is a definable set of skills and abilities. The only way you really know whether someone is leading is to observe what he or she is doing when in the act of leading.

This perspective is critical if you are going to become a better leader. This is because you can learn skills and behaviors. Skills can be broken down into teachable and learnable elements, and then learning experiences can be designed that, if done correctly and repeatedly, will generate behaviors that lead to improved performance.[4] Just in case you are wondering whether it's worth the effort, when we track the progress of people who participate in leadership development programs, we observe that they improve over time.[5] Furthermore, this improvement isn't a function of their personality type, their temperament, or their style. They learn to be better leaders as long as they engage in activities that help them learn how. The same thing is true for the other roles people play in organizations—and in life.

But here's the deal. Although leadership can be learned, not everyone learns it, and even all those who learn leadership don't master it. Why? There are many reasons, but chief among them is that you may not believe that you can. That's right. You may have bought into that myth that we talked about earlier— the one that says leadership is inherent and only a few people are blessed with the leadership gene. You may believe that leadership skill is something you are either born with or not, that it's fixed inside people or that some can learn to lead, but others cannot. You need to examine your mindset before you seriously set off on your learning leadership journey.

MIND YOUR MINDSET

Building your capacity to be a lifelong learner begins with what Carol Dweck, professor of psychology at Stanford University, calls a *growth mindset*. This mindset, she says, "is based on the belief that your basic qualities are things you can cultivate through your efforts."[6] Individuals who have a growth mindset believe people can learn to be better leaders—that they are made and not born.

She compares this with a *fixed mindset*—"believing that your qualities are carved in stone."[7] Those with the fixed mindset think that leaders are born and that no amount of training or experience is going to make them any better than they naturally are.

If you buy into the view that leaders are born and that talents are fixed at birth, it is highly unlikely that you'll put forth the time and effort to be better than you already are. It's also likely that you'll avoid challenges, give up quickly when things get tough, and perceive that spending any effort on training will be a general waste of time. You'll just wait for your talents to naturally blossom or hope somehow to be in the right place at the right time that match your skills.

On the other hand, if you begin with the belief that you can learn new skills no matter what your present level of competence is and that training and coaching will pay off, then you're much more likely to do whatever it takes to improve. You are more likely to seek and accept challenges, persist when obstacles are in your way or not be deferred when you have a setback, and see your efforts as necessary steps toward mastering leadership.

Mindsets also carry over into performance. In study after study, researchers have found that when working on business problems those individuals with fixed mindsets gave up more quickly and performed more poorly than those with growth mindsets.[8] The same is true for kids in school, athletes on the playing field, teachers in the classroom, and partners in relationships.[9]

Applying the concept of mindset to organizations, Carol and her colleagues found that in growth mindset companies, employees are "47 percent likelier to say that their colleagues are trustworthy, 34 percent likelier to feel a strong sense of ownership and commitment, 65 percent likelier to say that the company supports risk taking, and 49 percent likelier to say that the company fosters innovation."[10] Clearly, the mindset of organizational leaders can either facilitate or inhibit the growth of employees as well as the growth of the business.

Your beliefs about your ability to learn are where it all starts. They influence your motivation, your level of effort, your desire to persist, and your openness to feedback. If you believe that you can learn, it's significantly more likely that you will. If you believe that you can't learn, it's likely that you won't. As Carol points out, "For 20 years, my research has shown *the view you adopt for yourself* profoundly affects the way you lead your life. It can determine whether you become the person you want to be and whether you accomplish the things you value."[11]

Believing that you can lead and believing that you can learn to lead are essential to becoming a better leader. The good news is that research shows that you can learn to embrace a growth mindset.[12] Again, you just have to believe you can. So, mind your mindset.

THE KEY MESSAGE AND ACTION

The key message of this chapter is this: The best leaders are the best learners. They have a growth mindset. They believe that they are capable of learning and growing throughout their lives. To become a better leader, you must engage in continuous learning. You are never done learning, never done getting better. Continuous learning is a way of life. And it doesn't matter what your learning style is. What matters is how frequently you engage in learning activities. You can reflect, read, watch others, get a coach, attend some training, or just try out a new skill or technique. Whatever it is, engage in it every day.

SELF-COACHING ACTION

It's important that every day you take stock of what you've learned. You have to make learning leadership a daily habit— something we'll say more about later in this book. One way to establish that habit is to use your leadership journal to make notes at the end of each day—or each morning, if you prefer— to answer this one simple question: "What did I learn in the last 24 hours that will help me become a better leader?" It could be something about you, other people, the context in which you work, the external environment, a new technique, or anything else that contributes in some way to your knowledge, skills, and attitudes about leadership.

If you do this every day, you'll be amazed how much you've learned, and in the process, how much you've improved over time. You can also identify where you are stuck and how you may need to take some new path to get out of a rut.

CHAPTER 6

LEADERSHIP EMERGES FROM WITHIN

The primary instrument for leaders is the self. That's all leaders have to work with. It's not going to be code written by some brilliant programmer, apps on a smartphone, or clever phrases of a speechwriter that are going to make people better leaders. What leaders do with themselves makes the most difference. Mastery of the art of leadership comes from the mastery of the self. Ultimately, you will see, leadership development is self-development.

Authentic leadership flows from the inside out. It does not come from the outside in. Inside-out leadership is about discovering who you are, what compels you to do what you do, and what gives you the credibility to lead others. Inside-out leadership is about becoming the author of your own story and the maker of your own history. Inside-out leadership is also the only way to respond to what your constituents most want from you. And what is that? What they want to know is who you genuinely are.

Test this out for yourself. Imagine the following scenario. You're called to a conference room for a very important meeting. You and all your colleagues are sitting there, and in walks a person you've never met before. The individual begins to speak and says, "Hello. I'm your new leader." At the very moment you hear that announcement, what do you want to know about this person? What are the questions that immediately pop into your mind?

We've asked this question of many different groups around the world, and the most typical response is some variation of the question "Who are you?" For example, people say they want to ask a new leader:

- What do you stand for and believe in?
- What is your style?
- How do you make decisions?
- What makes you think you can do this?
- What makes you happy (or sad, frustrated, angry, etc.)?
- What qualifies you for this job?
- What have you done in the past?
- What do you like to do in your free time?
- To what extent do you think people are trustworthy?

Fundamentally, people want to know about *you*. They want to know about what inspires you, what drives you, what informs your decisions, what gives you strength, and what makes you who you are. They want to know about the person behind the title and position. They want to know what gives you the confidence to think that you can actually pull something off. They want to know about the person doing the leading before they're ever willingly going to become the people doing the following.

You can't expect to accomplish anything grand until you are aware of who you are and comfortable with being able to share yourself with others. If you're going to lead, then you have to wrestle with questions about what shaped you into the person you are now and what gives meaning to your leadership, your life, and your work.

We were sharing this observation in a workshop with individuals from a number of different organizations. One participant (Cheryl) said she could underscore just how important this point was by sharing her own experience related to a new vice president her organization had just hired. He was making the rounds with various teams, talking about his vision about what they needed to focus on. "The VP was visiting with us," Cheryl explained, "supposedly so that people could get to know him. Imagine how flabbergasted we were when someone asked him the question 'What do you like to do when you are not working?' and he replied, rather curtly, 'That's a personal matter and not relevant. Next question.'"

"But, that is the point, isn't it!" Cheryl exclaimed excitedly, and everyone listening to her story readily agreed. "We wanted, no we needed, to know: Who is this guy? What does he really care about? Why should we follow—believe and trust—him if we don't know who he is? And, he won't tell us!"

No one can put leadership into you. It's already there. You have to go find it inside of you and bring it out. The quest to become a leader, therefore, begins as an inner search to discover who you are. It's through this process of self-examination that you find the awareness needed to lead yourself and others.

THE THREE PERIODS OF SELF-DEVELOPMENT

An artist and educator friend of ours, Jim LaSalandra, after touring a retrospective of American painter Richard Diebenkorn's works, provided us some keen insights about the process of self-discovery. He told us, "There are really three periods in an artist's life. In the first, we paint exterior landscapes. In the second, we paint interior landscapes. In the third, we paint ourselves. That's when you begin to have your own unique style." What applies to the art of painting applies just as well to the art of leadership. When we look back over how leaders learn and grow, we see similar developmental stages.

Looking Out

When first learning to lead, you paint what you see on the outside of yourself—the exterior landscape. You read biographies and autobiographies about famous leaders. You observe what well-respected or famous leaders do, and you ask the advice of mentors. You read books and listen to podcasts and TED (Technology, Education, Design) talks by experienced executives and scholars. You participate in training programs. You accept job assignments so that you can work alongside someone who can coach you. You want to learn everything you can from others, and you often try to copy their style.

You do all this to learn the fundamentals and to acquire the tools and the techniques others have learned from their experience. Neither Bach nor Picasso sprang full-blown as Bach and Picasso; they needed models. The same is true for comedians, writers, athletes, and aspiring leaders. It's an absolutely essential period in any leader's development, and as an aspiring leader you can no more skip the fundamentals than can an aspiring painter or anyone learning a trade or craft.

Even though authenticity comes only when you find your own unique voice, sometimes when you're first developing your skills and abilities, it can be quite useful to read, observe, and imitate the practices of leaders you admire. If this is where you are in your leadership development process, take some time to do an inventory of who those leaders are. What do they do that you would like to do? Do you have some favorite leader biographies? What about favorite documentaries or movies about historical figures? What are the lessons about leadership you have learned from them? How about a supervisor you've had who's been particularly helpful to you? Maybe an athletic coach, a teacher, or a family member has given you some leadership guidance. Capture as much of this as you can, and take stock of what you've learned. Remember, the best leaders are the best learners, and they're constantly learning from others.

Don't worry about imitating someone else right now. It's about learning the fundamentals. You'll discover over time what fits you and what doesn't. As when trying on new clothes, you'll learn that on you some things look ridiculous and others make you sparkle.

Looking In

Somewhere along the way, though, you'll notice that your talks sound mechanical and rote, that your meetings are boring, and that your interactions feel terribly routine and empty. You'll awaken to the frightening thought that the words aren't yours, that the vocabulary is someone else's, and that the technique is right out of the textbook but not straight from the heart. Although you've invested so much time and energy in learning to do all the right things, you suddenly see that they're no longer serving you well. You may even feel like a phony, that you're faking it, and fear that you'll be seen as an imposter. In this regard, Kerry Ann Ostrea, accounting manager at Gilbane Federal, talked with us about how sometimes things might look right on the outside, but they are not just you—and you feel it on the inside. By way of example, she offered this analogy: "A dress might fit you perfectly in a dressing room, yet it just doesn't look right to you; it doesn't match with who you are. When you buy clothes, fashion or style is not the only consideration that matters. It must also fit the wearer."

When you look inside, as Kerry Ann says, does this fit right for you? In these moments, you begin to stare into the darkness of your inner territory and wonder what lies inside. You say to yourself, "I'm not someone else. I'm a unique human being. But, who exactly am I? What is my true voice?" For aspiring leaders, this awakening initiates a period of intense exploration, a period of testing, and a period of invention. You go beyond technique, training, imitating the masters, and taking the advice of others. You go through a period of exhausting experimentation, second-guessing, and anxious and even painful moments, to emerge from all those abstract strokes on the canvas to an expression of self that is truly your own.

For many people, reflecting on their personal-best leadership experiences was this sort of cathartic experience. Looking at their experience and thinking about their motivations and underlying values made them cognizant that leadership was not something outside of themselves that they needed to bring inside. In many ways, they already had much of what they needed to be a leader—in the present and into the future. It simply needed to be liberated from within.

The project Rich Howe, senior product line manager at NetApp, selected as his personal best was the most significant and memorable of his career until that point. Most important, he said, "I learned some hard lessons about myself, what I was capable of doing, and what I cared about." Anh Pham, engineering manager with Analog Devices Inc., said, "My personal best made me think rather deeply about what makes a good leader, and how I had those characteristics within myself." For some this was their first leadership experience, and they learned "so much," as Amy Drohan, senior customer success manager at ON24, explained, "This time changed my life. I am who I am and I am where I am in my life because of this experience."

Finding Your True Voice

The turning point in your development as a leader comes when you're able to merge the lessons from your outer and inner journeys. You awaken to the fact that you don't have to copy someone else, you don't have to read a script written by someone else, and you don't have to wear someone else's clothes. Because unless it's your words, and your style, then it's not really you; it's just an act: you pretending to be you. It was precisely this realization that Michael Janis, director of strategic marketing at Agilent Technologies, called "the most important lesson I've learned, and the one that is truly helping me move forward as a leader. After searching, seeking, and copying the behaviors of leaders in the hopes that I would somehow magically acquire their characteristics and talents, I've found that the truest strength in leadership comes from me, and who I am."

This leadership lesson is quite similar to what novelist and nonfiction writer Anne Lamott tells would-be writers in her classes: "The truth of your experience can only come through in your own voice. If it is wrapped in someone else's voice, we readers are suspicious, as if you are dressed up in someone else's clothes. You cannot write out of someone else's big dark place; you can only write out of your own. When you try to capture the truth of your experience in some other person's voice or on that person's terms, you are moving yourself one step further from what you have seen and what you know."[1]

What's true for writers is just as true for leaders. You cannot lead out of someone else's experience. You can only lead out of your own. Grant Hillestad recalled a transformative experience for him when he was involved with a college organization called Students Stay Leaders Forever. While participating in one of its community service road trips, he realized that he didn't need to worry about fitting in or acting cool because "it's just so much more important to be yourself. If you can trust in yourself, listen to and believe in yourself, you can be a leader and make a difference."

Grant found that realizing, and appreciating, who he truly was gave him the courage to navigate difficult situations and make tough choices. When his friends and other students said, "Are you nuts? You want me to *pay* to go and *work* during spring break?" Grant was able to stand up and speak confidently about how much the trips had meant to him, what had been accomplished, and "what I learned about myself." Like Grant, to lead others, you have to learn about yourself. After all, if you are to speak out, you have to know what to speak about, and if you are to stand up for your beliefs, you have to know the beliefs you stand for. To do what you say, you have to know what you want to say. Authentic leadership cannot come from the outside in. It comes from the inside out. In the next chapter we'll explore the critical conversation you must have with yourself to strengthen your true voice.

THE KEY MESSAGE AND ACTION

The key message of this chapter is this: No one can put leadership into you. Authentic leadership flows from the inside out. You have to liberate the capacity you already have, and that begins by taking an inner journey to discover who you are.

SELF-COACHING ACTION

Create a personal *lifeline* so that you can identify some of the key patterns in your life. What drives you down and what pulls you up? In your leadership journal, draw a horizontal line across the middle of the page. On the left-hand side of the page, write *Past*, and on the right-hand side, write *Present*. On the top half of the page, write *Peaks*, and at the bottom, write *Valleys*.

Now spend a few minutes recording on this chart significant events or experiences in your life. Start as far back as you'd like and continue to the present. If an event or experience was a peak—a high point, a significantly positive experience—put it above the line. If it was a valley—a low point, a significantly negative experience—put it below the line. Jot down a couple of words to identify what made each experience a peak. Next, make note of what motivated you to climb to each peak or the values that guided your decisions and actions along the way. Do the same thing for the valleys. Identify each and then indicate what motivated you to rise out of the valley or the values that guided you out of it.

Once you've done this, reflect on the themes or patterns you see in the peaks and in the valleys. Record the common motivations that emerge. Write down what some of your most important values are. Bottom line: What does this tell you about who you are, what your strengths are, and what matters most to you?

PART III

FUNDAMENTAL TWO: ASPIRE TO EXCEL

To become the very best leader you can be, you need to be clear about the core values and beliefs that guide your decisions and actions. You have to determine what you care most about and why it's important. Your motivation needs to be intrinsic and not instrumental. Top-performing leaders don't focus on making money, getting a promotion, or being famous. They want to lead because they care deeply about the mission and people they are serving.

People expect their leaders to be forward-looking. You have to be able to imagine what the future will be like to draw people forward. One place to start is by envisioning the kind of leader you'd like to be. This ideal image generates the emotional energy necessary to pull you forward.

Leadership is not just about you and about realizing only your values and vision. It's more about helping others realize theirs. Exemplary leaders and their constituents are in service of a larger purpose—a purpose beyond the self. Your success as a leader is inextricably linked to how successful you can make others.

In the next three chapters we take a look at these key themes on becoming an exemplary leader:

- You have to know what's important to you.
- Who you are now isn't who you will be.
- It's not just about you.

CHAPTER 7

YOU HAVE TO KNOW WHAT'S IMPORTANT TO YOU

Think about a historical leader that you admire, someone you could imagine following willingly. We've asked people around the world to answer this question, and all the individuals they identify are ones with strong beliefs about matters of principle. They all had unwavering commitment to a clear set of values. Similarly, the personal-best leadership cases we collected are, at their core, stories of individuals who remained true to deeply held values.

For Becky Schaar, technical program manager at Google, her personal-best reflection revealed the need to understand "what you deeply believe because people won't follow you, or even pay much attention to you, if you don't have strong beliefs." Olivia Lai, associate product strategist at Moody's Analytics (Hong Kong), recognized that "becoming a leader is a process of internal self-discovery. In order for me to become a leader and become an even better leader, it's important that I first define my values and principles. If I don't know what my own values are and determine expectations for myself, how can I set expectations for others?" Michael Gibler, when promoted to assistant manager at Seattle's Ultrazone, quickly grasped that to earn the respect of others, he needed to "be clear about my values." Nevzat Mert Topcu, who launched a Turkish magazine about computer games, told us that if you want to lead others, you have to get in touch with your core values: "You have to be honest with yourself in order to be honest with others."

Through their processes of self-discovery, Becky, Olivia, Michael, Nevzat, and many other leaders around the globe realized a fundamental lesson about leadership: To become an exemplary leader, you have to discover what is important to you, what you care about, and what you value. You can be the author of your own story and the maker of your own history only when you clarify the principles that you believe should guide you in your work and life. "I've come to understand that everyone has beliefs and values," was the poignant realization of yet another emerging leader, "and that in order for people to lead they've got to connect with them and be able to express them. I have to let people know and understand what my thoughts are so that I can become a good leader. How can others follow me if I'm not willing to listen to my inner self?" Indeed, remember that the very first person who has to follow you is you.

Have you ever walked into a place, or situation, and immediately gotten the sense that this wasn't right for you, that you didn't belong there, that this setting made you uncomfortable? Alternatively, have you ever just known that you belonged, that you could be yourself, that "This is a place that's right for me. This is a place I can stretch myself and learn new things." Of course you have; everyone has had those experiences. It's the same way in any group or job you might have. There comes a point when you recognize that it is, or is not, a good fit for who you are, your values, and your beliefs. You don't stick around a place very long, or make much of a commitment to a job, when you feel in your heart and in your soul that you don't belong. People who are clearest about what is important to them are better prepared to make choices based on personal principles rather than fads, Twitter retweets, or Facebook emojis and to be able to persist when the going gets tough. Commitment, the data show, is generally a function of just how clear you are about your personal values.[1]

People who aren't clear about what they believe in are likely to change their position with every new fashion or opinion poll and keep hitting the video reset button. Without core beliefs and with only shifting or temporary viewpoints, would-be leaders are judged as inconsistent and unreliable and disparaged for being political in their behavior. And when times get tough, they have nothing to guide them through uncertain or uncharted territory. Learning to be the best leader you can requires you to be clear about what you value and what you care enough about to be willing to make sacrifices, if necessary, to be sure that it's right, that it's working, that it's fair, that it's just, that it's safe, and that it's sustainable.

CLEAR VALUES INCREASE ENGAGEMENT

Your fundamental values and beliefs represent the core of who you are. They influence every aspect of your life: your moral judgments, the people you trust, the appeals you respond to, and the way you invest your time and your money. Values help you determine what to do and not to do. Lots of different interests out there compete for your time, your attention, and your approval. Before you listen to those voices, you have to listen to that voice inside that tells you what's truly important. Only then will you know when to say yes and when to say no. And mean it. Can you imagine being very capable of standing up for your beliefs when you're not clear about your personal values to begin with? How can you speak out if you don't know what's important to you? How can you have the courage of your convictions if you have no convictions? How can you stand up if you've nothing to stand upon? The leaders people admire the most, whether public figures or personal acquaintances, are those who had strong beliefs about matters of principle, an unwavering commitment to a clear set of values, and passion about their causes.

Tammy Levy decided to take a gap year after high school graduation and spend a year living in Israel, which stretched to three years before she returned to the United States. Those years in Israel, she said, forced her to think about herself as a person, along with her religious, political, and interpersonal beliefs: "It was a period of true introspection: a time during which I struggled and fought within myself to find myself." Following graduate school, and several years into her career, she reflected, "Throughout life I will continuously develop and learn. I will continue to introspect and question myself. Without this continuous inner fight I will not grow and will not learn." This is the journey every leader is on.

There's research suggesting there are as many as 125 values that people can hold.[2] You sure can't commit to all of them. You have to know which few are the most important to you. You have to know which ones you're willing to make sacrifices for—even die for if it comes to that. These choices are not necessarily easy, but they are necessary. You have to know in your gut that when you are making a decision, you are being true to who you are and what you stand for.

To get to that third stage of leadership development we discussed in Chapter 6—the stage where you are expressing your true voice—you have to commit yourself to a few enduring beliefs that will define you and test you. They are essential to knowing which way is north, south, east, or west. They serve as an inner compass by which you can navigate the course of your daily life and take the first steps along the journey to making a difference. It's easier to stay on the path you've chosen when you are clear about the signposts that will keep you oriented, or those that will be tangents and even likely dead ends. As Spencer Clark, then chief learning officer at Cadence Design Systems, explained to participants in one of our leadership development programs, "Knowing who I am has been enormously helpful in guiding me in making decisions about what to do and how I could do it."

This isn't mere theory or conjecture. We know from our research that people who are clearest about their personal values, for example, feel the strongest likelihood of achieving their life ambitions, are most willing to work long and hard, are most committed to their organizations, and feel less stress from work.[3] Clear personal values enable you to be more fully involved, focused, motivated, creative, and committed to your work. You feel empowered, willing to take initiative and move forward.

Being clear about your core beliefs doesn't just increase your engagement as a leader—it also has a significant impact on the engagement of your team members and the people around you. When direct reports strongly felt that their leaders were clear about their values and leadership philosophy, they in turn responded significantly more favorably to questions about their own sense of team spirit, pride in the organization, commitment to the organization's success, and willingness to work extra hard to meet organizational objectives. Asked about how much they trusted management, the people who rated their leaders as 'almost always' clear about their leadership philosophy indicated trust them over 66 percent more than those who said their leaders are "almost never" clear about their leadership philosophy. In addition, we found a significant correlation between the extent to which direct reports described their leaders' clarity around personal values and principles and how they rated these same leaders' effectiveness. You will find that people are able to be more focused and positive about their workplace when they work with leaders who know what they stand for.

The evidence is conclusive: You can be effective only when you are leading according to the principles that matter most to you. Otherwise, you are simply putting on an act, one that people can see through over time. When you have clarified your values and found your voice, you will have the inner confidence necessary to express ideas, choose a direction, make tough decisions, act with determination, and take charge of your life rather than impersonating others. It's also not surprising that work is more fulfilling and rewarding when it is consistent with your values.

VALUES-BASED LEADERSHIP SUSTAINS CAREER SUCCESS

What you value helps explain what motivates you to choose to join certain organizations and not others, follow a particular career path, or decide to pursue a new endeavor. Your values can also help explain why you are successful in those organizations and careers. One recent large-scale study offers powerful evidence of just how potent value orientations are.

One of the most comprehensive studies of the impact of internally based (also referred to in the study as values-based) motives was done with 10,000 U.S. Army leaders from the time they entered West Point, through their graduation, and then on into their careers as army officers and after.[4] This population represented 20 percent of the living graduates of the U. S. Military Academy. The ability to follow a single population over an extended period is rare, and the results of this study provide important information about the motivations that can lead to success in leadership after education and training.

The researchers first looked at what motivated individuals to enroll in The Academy. They administered a survey asking cadets to indicate the reasons why they chose to attend West Point. Of the reasons given, two types were of greatest interest. One type they referred to as *internal*, and the other they labeled *instrumental*. Internal motives were things such as "personal self-development," "desire to serve my country," and the "leadership training" they'd receive. Instrumental motives were things such as "to be able to get a better job," "reputation of West Point," and "to be able to make more money." Following graduation, the researchers studied academy graduates' performance as leaders in the military over a period of four to 10 years.

What they found was that "those with internal, intrinsic motives performed better than those with external, instrumental rationales for their service. We were surprised to find, however, that those with *both* internal and external rationales proved to be *worse* investments as leaders than those with fewer, but predominately internal, motivations. Adding external motivations didn't make leaders perform better." They further concluded that "Our study demonstrates that those who lead primarily from values-based motivations, which are inherently internal, outperform those who lead with additional instrumental outcomes and rewards."[5]

In other words, those cadets who made values-based decisions to join the military—decisions founded on becoming an outstanding officer—were more successful after graduation than those who joined to get a better job after leaving the military. Why you chose to do something in the first place can well determine whether you'll be successful at it years later. Success seems to follow those who engage in something because the endeavor has intrinsic value in itself and not because of the extrinsic rewards that will come from doing it. Deciding what you care about is a part of, and not apart from, being successful in your life and career. Studies of entrepreneurs show similar results: The missionaries outperform the mercenaries. Those with a mission to change the world are more successful than those who build to an exit strategy so that they can make lots of money.

There's another implication, albeit more subtle, of these research findings. Participating in any leadership development activity should be intrinsically important to you. Wanting to become the best leader you can be so that you can make a difference in the lives of others needs to be the reason for getting involved in education, training, and coaching. Contrary to conventional wisdom, participating for reasons such as getting a promotion, a pay raise, or a bonus may decrease your effectiveness.

Choose wisely. What you stand for and believe in today will influence not just who you are today but also how well you do tomorrow.

THE KEY MESSAGE AND ACTION

The key message of this chapter is this: You need to be clear about the core values and beliefs that guide your decisions and actions. You have to determine what you care most about and why it's important. To become the very best leader you can be, your motivation needs to be intrinsic and not instrumental. Top-performing leaders don't focus their attention on making money, getting a promotion, or being famous. They want to lead because they value making a difference and the mission they are serving.

SELF-COACHING ACTION

Imagine that you have the chance to take a six-month sabbatical, all expenses paid. You cannot take any work along on this

sabbatical. You will not be permitted to communicate with anyone at your office, agency, or plant during your absences—not
by letter, mobile phone, text message, e-mail, or other means.

Before you depart, however, you want to let the people you
work with know a few things to keep in mind during your
absence. For instance, you want to make sure they know the
principles you believe should guide their decisions and actions
in your absence—values about how they should treat one another, how they should work together, how they should deal
with conflicts, and so on.

Not permitted are lengthy reports, however: just a one-page
memorandum. Take this opportunity to write that memo in
your leadership journal.

CHAPTER 8

WHO YOU ARE ISN'T WHO YOU WILL BE

When you look back 10 years, are things the same today as they were then? And, when you look back those 10 years, are you doing now what you were doing then? We bet your answers to both questions are no.

Here are two more questions to consider: Looking ahead 10 years, do you expect the world to be different from what it is today? And, looking ahead 10 years from now, do you expect to be doing something different than you are doing today? To these questions, we'd bet your answers are yes. The point is obvious, isn't it?

Time passes. Contexts and people change. How the world will be in the future is likely to be different from how it is in the present or was in the past. Who you will be in the future is also likely to be different than who you are now or were in the past. Although this statement may seem so transparent and simple, it's crucial that you appreciate just how significant this observation is.[1] It gets to the very essence of what leaders do, and a big part of that is influencing just what the future will be like five, 10, or 20 years down the road. It forces you to ask and answer for yourself such questions as: What do I want the world to be like in 10 years? What are my aspirations for my future? What can I do to help create that future? What can I do to influence the future direction in which other people head? What kind of a person, and leader, do I want to become?

THE DOMAIN OF LEADERS IS THE FUTURE

The capacity to imagine the future is a fundamental defining characteristic of human beings, separating *Homo sapiens* from other species. And the ability to imagine exciting future possibilities is also a defining competence of leaders. We've surveyed thousands of people worldwide on what they want in their leaders, and they tell us that being *forward-looking* (visionary, foresighted, concerned about the future, and having a sense of direction) is second only to *honesty* as their most admired leader quality. On average, 71 percent of U.S. respondents select it. In Asia, Europe, and Australia the preference for forward-looking is a full 10 percentage points higher. At the most senior level in organizations, *forward-looking* is selected nearly 90 percent of the time.[2]

Being forward-looking is not the same as meeting the impending deadline for your current project. Whether that project ends three months, one year, five years, or 10 years down the road, the leader's job is to think beyond that end date. The leader has to think about "What will we be doing *after* the project is completed?" If you're not thinking about what's happening *after* the completion of your longest-term project, then you're thinking only as long term as everyone else. In other words, your perspective is redundant! As a leader, you need to be thinking about the next project, and the one after that, and the one after that.

Developing your leadership capacity will require you to spend considerably more time thinking about the future than you are now doing, and orienting your actions in real time more toward that future than simply responding to things that have happened in the past or are happening right now. Being reactive only gets you back to the status quo; being proactive is what gets you ahead.

Another crucial question to ask is "What's better?" What's better than what you (personally or organizationally) are now doing or anticipate doing in the future? This question necessarily propels you forward in your thinking. An essential ingredient in people's willingness to put in the time and energy needed to make extraordinary things happen is helping them find meaning and purpose in their current situations by focusing on making life better in the long run.[3]

Despite the general importance that people place on being forward-looking, be sensitive to two challenges. The first is that younger respondents, as well as those with limited work experience, don't place as much importance on the quality of forward-looking as do their older and more experienced colleagues. Leaders in their early twenties and on the front lines tend to value forward-looking 20 percentage points less than middle-level managers and about 40 percentage points less than C-suite executives. The appreciation of forward-looking as a desirable leader attribute grows over time and with increasing responsibilities. You need to get ahead of this curve by starting now to develop your capacity to think longer term.

The second challenge, according to our data, is that people report that they're not as good at or as comfortable with envisioning the future or enlisting others as they are with the other leadership practices.[4] The feedback from their colleagues and direct reports is the same. The skill set at which the vast majority of leaders need to become significantly more capable is inspiring a shared vision. These findings mean that you'll have to be even more deliberate in learning to look ahead and talk about the future. Because there are probably lots of other demands on your time, this means you'll need to make very concerted efforts to become more oriented to the future—to what's not going on that should be, to what could be, or to what must be happening if things are going to be better than they are today. As the National Hockey League's all-time leading point scorer, Wayne Gretzky, put it, "A good hockey player plays where the puck is. A great hockey player plays where the puck is going to be."

TO SEE INTO THE FUTURE, BE MINDFUL IN THE PRESENT

The daily pressures, the pace of change, the complexity of problems, and the turbulence in global marketplaces can often hold your mind hostage and make you think that you have neither the time nor the energy to be more future oriented. But attending to the future doesn't have to be in addition to everything else you are already busy doing. As counterintuitive as it might seem, the best place to start creating the future is by being more mindful in the present.

The failure of not being forward-looking may be more because of being mind*less* in the present than any other factor. You've got to get off automatic pilot, not noticing what's going on around you, believing that you know everything you need to know, viewing the world through preestablished categories, and operating from a single point of view. You aren't present at all. Your body may be in the room, but your mind has been turned off. To increase your ability to conceive of new and creative solutions to today's problems, you have to *stop*, *look*, and *listen*.

You have to *stop doing* for some amount of time each day. Create some white space on your calendar. You have to remind yourself that the disruptive electronic devices have an off switch. Turn off the mobile phone, the text messaging, the e-mail, the smart watch, and the browser. Stop being in motion. Stop the distractions. Then start noticing more of what's going on around you right now. To see things, you have to be present, you have to pay attention, and you have to be curious.

Look around. Most innovation comes more from noticing what's going on in the here and now rather than gazing into some crystal ball. The best leaders are and have been those who are the keenest observers of the human condition. They just pay more attention than everyone else does to all that's around them. So, see what you can do to begin looking at the familiar in novel ways. Look for differences and distinctions. Look for patterns. Look at things from multiple perspectives. Look for unmet needs.

And *listen.* Listen to the weak signals. Listen to what's not said. Listen to the unheard voices. Listen to the people who are not like you. Listen for things you've never heard before.

When you stop, look, and listen, you will be amazed at all the possibilities around you. Leaders often find their way to the future because they tend to be restless, never quite satisfied with the status quo. And no matter how well things may be going, leaders believe that they could be even better. Most often, they fix things before they break.

ENVISIONING THE FUTURE

Envisioning the future typically begins with a vague desire to do something that would challenge yourself and others. As the desire grows in intensity, so does your determination. The strength of this internal energy forces you to clarify what it is that you most want to do and what you care about most deeply. You begin to get a sense of what you want the product, process, service, team, or organization to look like, feel like, and be like when you and others have completed the journey. You may even try sketching out or writing down your image of the future or drawing a model of it.

Because you want what you create to be unique, you differentiate your organization or cause from others that produce the same product, provide the same service, or make the same promise. Yours is a distinctive vision, you believe. It's also ideal. After all, you want to set a new standard of perfection, beauty, or excellence. You want yours to be a model for others. And just because it may only be an image of the future, not something yet fully developed or even capable of a detailed description, this doesn't mean you can't move ahead. It's like driving at night with the headlights on. You may be able to see only a short distance ahead, but you can make the whole journey in that fashion. Leaders have an ideal and unique image of the future, or what's popularly referred to as a vision.

Visions for organizations, reformations, and movements, as well as visions for journeys, are more complicated than this, of course. And you don't necessarily follow a sequential process for clarifying your vision—especially if you're attempting to achieve what no one has ever achieved before. The pioneers in any endeavor have no maps to study, no guidebooks to read, and no pictures to view. They can only imagine the possibilities. As it was with the Vikings preparing for their first voyage, explorers can only dream. Without any previous experience to guide them, the first ones to explore may find that their dreams are fantasies or that their visions are much harder to attain than they had expected.

On the plus side, however, the lack of previous experience means that pioneers can make up the future that they wish to create or discover. Those in earlier centuries who set out in search of new lands were often not very realistic: Their boats were small and their provisions meager. But that lack of realism didn't deter them from making the journey; in fact, it helped. Their dreams of what was possible fueled their enthusiasm and better enabled them to persuade others that many interests would be served.

YOUR IDEAL SELF

Visions of the future are not predictions. They are creations. No one can say what the future will be with 100 percent certainty. There are too many factors to consider. However, you can say what you would *like* the future to be. And the place to start that conversation is to focus first on the kind of leader *you* would like to be in the future.

Becoming an exemplary leader fundamentally changes who you are. It changes your relationship with yourself. You're no longer just an individual contributor. You're now someone who takes people on journeys to places they've never been.

Becoming a leader changes how you present yourself day in and day out. You are expected to be a role model for the values that you and the organization espouse.

It changes how you see the future. You are expected to be able to imagine exciting future possibilities and communicate them to others.

It changes how you respond to challenges. You are expected to be comfortable with uncertainty, champion experimentation, and learn from experiences.

It changes how you relate to others. You are expected to build relationships, foster collaboration, strengthen others, and forge trust.

It changes how you show others that you appreciate them. You are expected to genuinely recognize contributions and celebrate team successes.

Being true to these expectations and leading with your best self means that you need to be clear and comfortable with the kind of leader you want to become. We'll get to the ideal image of the future for the *common good* in the next chapter, but research has shown that the "emotional driver of intentional change" comes from your ideal self.[5] It's the generator that arouses the positive emotion you need to keep moving forward.

THE KEY MESSAGE AND ACTION

The key message of this chapter is this: People expect their leaders to be forward-looking. This quality differentiates between leaders and individual contributors. To look toward the future, you start by being mindful of the present. Stop, look, and listen to what is happening around you. That way you'll be better attuned to your own and others' aspirations. The ability to draw people forward requires you to be able to imagine what the future will look, sound, and feel like. One place to start is envisioning the kind of leader you'd like to be in five, 10, or 20 years. This ideal image of self generates the necessary emotional energy to pull you forward.

SELF-COACHING ACTION

Imagine that 10 years from now you have been honored as the Leader of the Year. You are attending a ceremony in your honor. One after another, colleagues and coworkers, members of your family, and good friends take the stage and talk about your leadership and how you have made a positive difference in their lives. What do you hope they will say about you? How do you hope people will remember you on that day? This exercise isn't about going on an ego trip; it's about reflecting deeply on the legacy you want to leave. In your leadership journal record your thoughts about your L.I.F.E.:

Lessons: What vital *lessons* do you hope others will say you
have passed on? For example, she taught me how to face
adversity with grace and determination.

Ideals: What *ideals*—values, principles, and ethical standards—
do you hope people will say you stood for? For example,
he stood for compassion and service to others.

Feelings: What *feelings* do you hope people will say they have/
had when being with you or when thinking about you? For
example, she always made me feel I was capable of doing
the impossible.

Expressions: What lasting *expressions* or contributions—tangible
and intangible—will people say that you left to them and
to others yet to come? For example, you can see his legacy
in the thousands of young people he taught, who went on
to achieve great things.

Review what you wrote, and as you do so identify some
central themes. Come back to your L.I.F.E. periodically, at least
annually, to review and update it. In addition, use this analysis
to help inform the kinds of development you need to become
the ideal leader you imagine yourself to be on the night they
honor you!

CHAPTER 9

IT'S NOT JUST ABOUT YOU

P eople constantly ask us, "How do you define leadership?" Although we have our definition, before responding we usually turn the question back to the audience and ask, "What do you think is the simplest answer to that question? What's the easiest way to know if someone is a leader or not?"[1]

Invariably, the answer we get is some version of this: "They have followers." That's the aha moment. It is followers who define whether someone is a leader. There can't be any leaders if there aren't any followers. If you are marching forward toward a future destination and you turn around and notice that no one is there, then you're just out for a stroll. Leadership is fundamentally a relationship between those who aspire to lead and those who would choose to follow, and if no one is following you, then there's no relationship there. There's nothing that connects what you see to what they want. This is true regardless of whether that relationship is one to one or one to many.

Don't get hung up about being *the* leader. Even though Alan Daddow, at that time, was the person in charge at Elders

Pastoral in Western Australia, he understood that his "responsibility was doing whatever I could to maximize the team's effectiveness." Repeatedly, upon reflecting on their personal-best leadership experiences, people appreciated that it "wasn't about me; it was about us." As Sunil Menon, research and development (R&D) director with Avaya, pointed out, "Leaders know that they need partners to make extraordinary things happen. They invest actively and heavily in building trustworthy relationships." Like Alan and Sunil, you need to appreciate that success can be achieved only if you make everyone else in the organization successful at doing what they need to accomplish. People won't follow you for very long, if at all, if your message is "I want you to help me become successful." They will follow you when your message is "I am here to help us all be successful in serving a common cause."

Appreciating that leadership doesn't happen without having followers is humbling. It's a reminder that leadership is not all about you, the leader. It's not only about your vision or about your values. Leadership is about *shared* vision and values. It's about getting everyone aligned with a common purpose, a common cause.

The impact of this reciprocal relationship is quite profound. Would it surprise you to know that when people don't feel valued and appreciated by their manager or supervisor, they are more than four times more likely to look for another job compared with those who report strong relationships with their managers? Alternatively, does it surprise you to know that most managers fail in their careers because of poor relationships with their direct reports?[2]

Of course, no relationship can begin until people start talking and sharing information with one another; and someone has to go first in this process. You should be the one to go first in sharing yourself with others because that helps build trust. But nothing extraordinary happens if no one is willing to go second or third and so on.

YOU HAVE TO SEE WHAT OTHERS SEE

In his famous speech during the August 28, 1963, Great March on Washington, Martin Luther King Jr. exclaimed, "I have a dream." This dream involved images of the future: "On the red hills of Georgia, the sons of former slaves and the sons of former slave owners will be able to sit down together at the table of brotherhood." "One day right there in Alabama, little black boys and black girls will be able to join hands with little white boys and white girls as sisters and brothers." "When we allow freedom to ring, when we let it ring from every village and every hamlet, from every state and every city, we will be able to speed up that day when *all* of God's children, black men and white men, Jews and Gentiles, Protestants and Catholics, will be able to join hands . . ."

He also said, "This is our hope," and exclaimed that the dream would not be realized unless "We are willing to work together, we are willing to struggle together, to go to jail together."[3] Those gathered at the Lincoln Memorial that day cheered Dr. King's message not merely because he was a dynamic speaker. They cheered and applauded because they could relate to the dream as their own. It was their hopes and aspirations he was speaking about, not just his own. They could see what he saw because he could see what they imagined.

Although you need to be clear about your vision and values, you must also be attentive to those around you. If you can't find alignment between what you care about and what others care about, then you won't find a common purpose or achieve much success. Almost no one likes being told, "Here is where we're going, so get on board with it"—no matter how dressed up it is in all kinds of fine and fancy language. They want you to be able to hear what they have to say, and they want to see themselves in the picture that you are painting. "What's in it for me?" is a fair and reasonable question.

This means that to become the best leader you can be, you have to know deep down what *others* want and need. You have to understand *their* hopes, *their* dreams, *their* needs, and *their* interests. You have to know your constituents, and you have to relate to them in ways they will find engaging.

YOU HAVE TO CONNECT WITH OTHERS

The kind of communication needed to enlist others in a common purpose requires understanding people at a much deeper level than you may normally find comfortable. It requires understanding others' strongest yearnings and their deepest fears. It requires a profound awareness of their joys and their sorrows. It requires experiencing life as they experience it.

Being able to do this is not magic, nor is it rocket science. It's all about listening very, very carefully to what other people want. Nevertheless, what do you do if people can't articulate what it is that they want? What if people don't know what they need? That's even more reason to be a stellar listener. Listening is not just about the words; it's about paying attention. It's about what is unspoken. It's about reading between the lines. It's about noting what makes them smile, what gets them angry, how they spend their time (and not just at work), and so on. However, from a leadership perspective, what you can be sure of is that everyone wants a tomorrow that is better than today. They don't necessarily all want the same thing, but they all want it to be an improvement.

We can't emphasize this enough: Leadership is a relationship. Still, many people believe that you shouldn't get too close to other people in an organizational context because this will not only cloud your judgment about them but also interfere with your ability to make hard and challenging (or unpopular) decisions that affect them.

Sergey Nikiforov, now vice president and chief evangelist at enterprise software solutions company GOAPPO, earlier in his career told us that he "blindly followed this sort of advice for a few years without giving it too much thought." One day, however, he decided to find out what impact "normal human contact" with people in his workplace would have. Therefore, he sent a note out to the technical staff and invited them to have dinner together at a local restaurant if their schedule permitted it. He came to the restaurant a little early and waited at an empty table with anticipation, wondering whether anybody would come, thinking that they might be suspicious of why he had asked them to get together in such an informal atmosphere, outside their traditional offices. Eventually, one by one, his colleagues started to arrive. Sergey said:

> We sat there in awkward silence, staring at our menus
> for a few minutes, until I finally decided to come clean.
> I told them there was no specific job-related reason why
> we were getting together. All I wanted to do was to
> break down those boss–subordinate barriers, and get to
> know them better. I knew them as specialists very well,
> but I had only a faint idea of what these people were
> outside of work. I did not know much about them. I
> apologized, and explained that I hoped they would treat
> this dinner as a sign of goodwill, as a hand extended
> forward to welcome them as individuals, and not as tech-
> nical minds.
>
> It turns out they had similar thoughts about me as
> well: My subordinates knew me as a boss, and a special-
> ist, but were rather uncertain about what kind of person

I was outside of the company. We talked for four straight hours that evening! They were eager to share their personal lives, aspirations, hobbies, vacation plans, and a thousand other things. As I listened to them through the night, I realized how handicapped I was before without being connected with my colleagues at a personal level; how limiting my messages must have been without the benefit of a personal contact.

Sergey discovered that such a simple thing as hanging out at a dinner could help him find common ground with his colleagues, enabling them to listen to each other, as he said, "with open hearts."

Finding common ground is what enables you to have something upon which to build. It creates the platform for constructing a better future. Understanding your colleagues in this way allows you to know whether the future you want to create will be a future others will want to live and work in. For example, recent research has found that millennials strongly favor work–life balance. They are quite willing to work hard and to undertake challenging assignments—in fact, they desire them—but they also want more personal time, more time with friends and family than prior generations expressed. Although it's not true of every millennial, most rank work–life balance ahead of status and money.[4] Their boomer parents, on the other hand, rated work ahead of family life. Regardless of the generational cohort you are working with, enlisting others in a shared vision of the future requires that you understand their needs. To do that, you need to get to know your key constituents individually.

Connecting deeply with others enables leaders to appreciate what drives the people around them and what unites them. Leadership becomes a dialogue and not a monologue. It becomes a conversation and not a recitation.

YOU HAVE TO SERVE A LARGER PURPOSE

There's a lot written about leadership that gives the impression that people only want to follow individuals endowed with charismatic qualities. This theory leaves the impression that to become a leader, you need to possess personal magnetism or develop the ability to charm and persuade, and then people will automatically follow you. Not so.

People want to follow a meaningful purpose, not simply do some work in exchange for cash. If you want to lead others, you have to put principles and purpose ahead of everything else. The larger mission is what calls everyone, leader and constituent alike, forward. It's what gives significance to the hard work required to do anything extraordinary.

Meaningful work is vital to full engagement. We find in our research that when people say they feel like they are making a difference in their organizations, their engagement scores are substantially higher than when they feel they aren't making a difference. Other researchers have similarly noted, "Employees who derive meaning and significance from their work were more than three times as likely to stay with their organizations—the highest single impact of any variable in our survey. These employees also reported 1.7 times higher job satisfaction and they were 1.4 times more engaged in their work."[5]

There's a very substantial benefit to learning when you can find meaning in the work that you do. Whether it's learning to lead, learning to write computer code, or learning how to provide excellent customer service, having a self-transcendent purpose significantly enhances one's dedication to learning. Having a goal that has the potential to "have some effect on or connection to the world beyond the self" increases both your involvement and persistence in learning. Because of your more intense involvement, you will also be more likely to resist the temptation to engage in other pursuits even when whatever you are doing is boring.[6] Learning to lead can be challenging and difficult and perhaps even tedious at times. Knowing that you are engaged in something that is bigger than you are, something that will improve the lives of your colleagues, customers, family, friends, or citizens of the world, makes the difficult challenges of both leading and learning a bit easier to overcome.

Research also shows that viewing your work as a calling as compared to seeing it as a job or a career leads to the highest levels of satisfaction with both your work and your life. Having a calling also connects to better health.[7] Finding meaning and purpose in work has benefits that go well beyond a paycheck and profits. Becoming an exemplary leader is a very rewarding experience, one that brings with it not only a sense of accomplishment but also a feeling of worthiness and being of service to others.

THE KEY MESSAGE AND ACTION

The key message of this chapter is this: Leadership is not simply about you and realizing only your values and vision. It's more about helping others achieve theirs. For leaders and constituents alike, putting out discretionary energy requires that people feel their efforts are serving a larger purpose beyond the self. Your success as a leader links inextricably to how well you understand others' hopes, dreams, and aspirations. You have to find common ground with your constituents, and doing that means connecting with what gives their lives meaning and purpose.

SELF-COACHING ACTION

In your leadership journal make a list of your key relationships. Include your team members, your manager, important internal and external customers, peers you often collaborate with, and anyone else with whom you are interdependent. If the list is too long, start with people with whom you have the most frequent contact. For each individual, ask yourself:

• What are the values that this person holds dear?
• What are his or her standards?
• What are his or her future hopes and aspirations?
• What is the higher-order purpose that gives this person's work and life meaning?

It's likely that you won't be able to answer all of these questions for everyone on your list—and even if you can, you might want to verify your assumptions with them. Schedule an informal face-to-face conversation. Tell them that you are genuinely interested in what they value and look for in their workplace, and career, and want to talk to them about it. It might go more smoothly if you give them some questions in advance because this kind of conversation can require some thoughtful preparation. Make sure the tone of the conversation is casual; this is not really an interview and certainly not an interrogation. It's also likely that they'll want to hear your own answers to these questions—so be prepared—but share in a way that keeps the focus on the other person and not on you.

Once you've recorded your answers, step back from the data. See whether you notice any patterns. What are the common themes in the responses that give you clues about a possible shared vision that unites everyone?

PART IV

FUNDAMENTAL THREE: CHALLENGE YOURSELF

To develop as a leader and do your best, you have to step outside your comfort zone. You have to seek new experiences, test yourself, make some mistakes, and keep climbing back up that learning curve.

You have to be curious, taking the initiative to try new things and experimenting with novel ideas and new ways of doing things. And when you do so, you are inevitably going to make mistakes and fail. The key is drawing lessons from the experience and repeating the cycle of learning.

To get better at leading, you have to get gritty. You have to persist in the face of difficulties, thinking more like a marathoner than a sprinter. Everyone stumbles in the process of developing, so don't let this sidetrack or dissuade you. Bounce forward from the setbacks. Strengthen your resilience.

It takes courage to learn. When you challenge yourself, it's likely that you'll be doing things that scare you. There will be fear and uncertainty, so you need to see yourself making a choice about how to move forward, finding meaning and purpose in setting off in a new direction.

In the next four chapters we take a look at these key themes on becoming an exemplary leader:

- Challenge is your leadership training ground.
- Get curious and go kick the ball around.
- Get gritty, and stay hardy.
- Courage gives you the strength to grow.

CHAPTER 10

CHALLENGE IS YOUR LEADERSHIP TRAINING GROUND

My absolute favorite thing about human beings, said Kaily Adair, an honors business student and Phi Mu at the University of Alabama, "is that we're never satisfied with our condition—in the sense that we are constantly questioning, exploring, and innovating in order to better our situation as a whole." Kaily's observation expresses one of the most important truths about leadership—the truth that challenge is the crucible for greatness.[1] We said this in Chapter 1, and we're going to say more about it here. No leader ever made anything extraordinary happen by keeping things the same.

Kaily also added that:

> If we were just content with the way things were, we might not have ever gotten past the Stone Age, we might never have discovered a way to harness electricity, and we may never have created the Internet enabling people around the world to connect. We are now researching ways to cure cancer, put people on Mars, and perfect

alternative energy technologies—each day getting one step closer to what was considered science fiction less than a century ago. Better yet, once we achieve this, we will be searching for the next area for growth. We are constantly looking to challenge the process.

Ginni Rometty, IBM's chair, president, and chief executive officer (CEO), would likely agree with Kaily. At the 2015 *Fortune* Most Powerful Women Summit, she offered this advice: "Think of when did you ever learn the most in your life? What experience? I guarantee you'll tell me it was a time you felt at risk."[2]

To become a better leader, you have to step out of your comfort zone. You have to challenge the conventional ways of doing things and search for opportunities to innovate. Exercising leadership not only requires you to challenge the organizational status quo but also requires you to challenge your internal status quo. You have to challenge *yourself.* You have to venture beyond the boundaries of your current experience and explore new territory. Those are the places where there are opportunities to improve, innovate, experiment, and grow. Growth is always at the edges, just outside the boundaries of where you are right now.

Challenging yourself doesn't mean you need to go out and start something entirely new, launch a new company, begin a social movement, or change history to be considered a leader. But you do have to be involved in exploring, investigating, and experimenting with how things could be better than they are now. Just take a look around today's homes, neighborhoods, and workplaces, and you can't help noticing lots of things that aren't going as well as they could. There are no shortages of opportunities to improve the way things are and to have the possibility of making a difference.

PEOPLE DO THEIR BEST WHEN CHALLENGED

Challenge is the defining context for leadership. We've consistently found this to be the case in our research on what people are doing when performing at their personal best as leaders. And not only is it the context for leadership, but it's also the context for learning.

In Chapter 3, we described the Personal-Best Leadership case study, the research methodology we use in our investigations of what people do when performing at their best as leaders. We explained that after reviewing thousands of these cases, we concluded that (1) everyone had a leadership story to tell, and (2) the leadership actions and behaviors across these stories were quite similar. The pattern of those responses led to the discovery of The Five Practices of Exemplary Leadership.

We concluded something else from these cases of leadership best practices: Every one of them was about change, challenge, and adversity. In their Personal-Bests, people described dealing with misfortune, with turbulence, and with unexpected difficulties and hardships. They told us about venturing out into unchartered waters—personally, professionally, and organizationally. They told us about having to turn around failing operations or starting up a brand-new venture. They told us about pioneering a project no one else would even try or being the first to tackle an issue that terrified others. Not one single story was about keeping things the same, doing things the way they are always done, or maintaining the status quo. Not one.

Our research shows that:

- Opportunities to challenge the status quo and introduce change open the door to doing one's best. Challenge is the motivating environment for excellence.

- Challenging opportunities often bring forth skills and abilities that people don't know they have. Given opportunity and support, time and again ordinary people can get extraordinary things done in organizations.
- People who become leaders don't always seek the challenges they face. Challenges also seek leaders.

It's important also to remember that we asked people to tell us about their personal-best leadership experiences. We didn't ask them to talk to us about change, or hardship, or turbulence, or volatility, or first ever, or adversity. But that's what they discussed, and that is why we say that challenge is the crucible for greatness. Maintaining the status quo is the breeding ground for mediocrity.

Mihaly Csikszentmihalyi, distinguished professor of psychology and management and founder and codirector of the Quality of Life Research Center at Claremont Graduate University, found something similar in researching *flow*—a state in which a person is completely immersed in an activity and it seems quite effortless. It's often referred to as being in the zone. What he found was that "The best moments in our lives are not the passive, receptive, relaxing times. . . . The best moments usually occur when a person's body or mind is stretched to its limits in a voluntary effort to accomplish something difficult and worthwhile."[3] It's not only personal-best leadership that comes from stretching ourselves to do something that's difficult; everything that truly makes people happy in life comes from this kind of experience.

If you are going to learn to lead, then you need to be restless when it comes to the status quo, adopt the leadership attitude of looking for opportunities to challenge your skills and abilities, and be willing to experiment with changing the business-as-usual environment. Good enough can never be good enough when you strive to be the best you can be. In fact, we find that the more people report that they actively search outside the boundaries of their organizations for innovative ways to improve what is going on, the more effective and engaged they feel in their workplaces. And their managers and colleagues see this action, along with seeking out challenging opportunities to test one's skills and abilities, as directly correlated with how favorably they evaluate that individual's effectiveness.[4]

CHALLENGE INTRODUCES YOU TO WHAT'S IMPORTANT

Challenges, difficulties, setbacks, and hardships are all familiar sights on the leadership landscape. And one of the things they cause you to do is to come face-to-face with yourself. They are a rather harsh way of reminding you of what's most important to you, what you value, and where you want to go. Randy Pausch knew this all too well when he delivered his now-famous last lecture at Carnegie Mellon University. At the very beginning of his speech, Randy stunned the audience when he told them that he had numerous tumors in his liver and that his doctors said he had three to six months of good health left. But he quickly added, "We cannot change the cards we're dealt, just the way we play the hand." He said that he was not feeling morose or in denial and that he was well aware of what was happening to him. Then, in the course of his lecture, he made this observation: "The brick walls are there for a reason. They are not there to keep us out. The brick walls are there to give us a chance to show how badly we want something."[5]

Randy's personal circumstances were certainly unique to him, but his observation applies to everyone. It's especially relevant to leaders. Your challenges may at times seem insurmountable compared with those others face. But you have to remind yourself that many generations before you have success-fully dealt with world wars, economic depressions, and natural disasters. They've had to adapt to technological innovations, scientific advancements, and cultural shifts. What might seem like brick walls are really doors to a new future, asking, "What do you want? And how badly do you want it?"

Challenge, whether it's overcoming adversity or creating something unique and new, presents you the chance to ask yourself some very fundamental questions about your purpose and direction. It's another reason, as we discussed in Chapter 7, why it's essential to know what's important to you.

TO GROW, SEEK CHALLENGING OPPORTUNITIES

Leadership scholar Warren Bennis has said that "Leaders learn by leading, and they learn best by leading in the face of obsta-cles. As weather shapes mountains, problems shape leaders. Difficult bosses, lack of vision and virtue in the executive suite, circumstances beyond their control, and their own mistakes have been the leaders' basic curriculum."[6] Practitioner Jeanne Rineer, a group manager of camera procurement at Apple, agrees. Leaders, she says, "look for innovative ways to improve by taking risks and experimenting. If failures and mistakes are made, the mistakes are looked upon as learning opportunities instead of patterns of incompetence."

Recent studies on the state of leadership and executive development reinforce Warren's observations and Jeanne's experience. In one survey, executives reported that they felt the most effective methods for leadership development were action-learning projects and stretch assignments.[7] In another study, activities such as participating in cross-functional teams, working on a team to solve a specific customer issue, or being part of a global project team were the kinds of experiences that were most effective in developing their leadership capabilities.[8] Just as leaders have to search for opportunities inside and outside their organizations to grow and develop the business, learners have to find those same kinds of opportunities to improve themselves. It's clear that if you want to develop your leadership capabilities, you need to take the initiative and volunteer for assignments that stretch you beyond your current comfort zone. You need to make them part of your personal leadership development curriculum. The only way that you can learn is when you are doing things that you've never done before. If you do only what you already know how to do, then you will never develop new skills and competencies, nor develop the confidence that comes with increased competence.

Remember, however, that a learning curve is not a straight line.[9] Let's say you're doing something right now that you know how to do, and you're doing it very well. Then people like us come along and suggest that there's a need to improve and to learn new things. Because you're eager to excel, you say, "Great. I don't know how to do this, and I'd like to learn." But when you engage in learning, instead of getting better, your performance at the beginning typically declines. That's why it's called a learning *curve*. When learning something new, performance almost always goes *down* before it goes up—and if it doesn't go down, then you are only doing something you already know how to do.

Abigail Donahue, a development associate at National Writing Project, experienced that learning curve when given the opportunity to convene a session at her organization's national conference. She said that it was "possibly one of the most challenging things I've done and stretched me to my limits in organizing this." In the past when she didn't get something right at the beginning, she would typically doubt her capabilities and take that as a sign to stop doing whatever she was doing. However, Abby was able to find "an internal reservoir of strength to keep going because of the realization that learning is not a linear process. You are going to make some mistakes, but you just need to pick yourself up, learn from them, and keep moving forward."

Perhaps, you've been told more than once in your life to "get it right the first time." That's sound advice if it's a perfected method and you're concerned about consistency and quality. But it's terrible advice if you're trying to learn new things. The fact is that when learning something brand-new, no one ever gets it right the first, or second, or even possibly the third time. You're going to make mistakes while learning. That's just a natural part of the learning process, as Abby came to appreciate.

The real issue is how *fast* can you learn? How quickly can you learn from your mistakes and your failures before you get it right? Picture that learning curve in your head, and know that innovations are nearly always failures before they are successes. If every inventor, entrepreneur, or leader quit halfway through, nothing new would ever happen. Each failure produces valuable lessons that can be applied to the next iteration. Perseverance is an essential characteristic of exemplary learners, as well as of exemplary leaders. William J. Stribling, director and screenwriter, told us that "Embracing and loving failure is one of the most valuable things I've learned. It sucks, and it's hard every time, but ultimately it leads to good things and a richer perspective." He went on to say that failure and success are all about perspective and related how impressed he is by the abilities of baseball managers and players to embrace failure. They play 162 games in a year, and winning slightly more than half of those games is a great success. A player might hit the ball only 25 percent of the time, and that's considered a solid batting average. As Will relates, "Having faith in yourself and your abilities allows you to accept the very real (and likely) possibility of failure, making failure far less scary, and, in fact, necessary." Failures and disappointments are inevitable in learning and life. How you handle them will ultimately determine your effectiveness and success. You have to be honest with yourself and with others. You have to own up to your mistakes and reflect on your experiences so that you gain the learning necessary to be better the next time around.

THE KEY MESSAGE AND ACTION

The key message of this chapter is this: To both do your best and develop as a leader, you have to challenge yourself and face challenges head-on. You have to step outside your comfort zone. You have to seek new experiences, test yourself, climb over brick walls, experiment, make some mistakes, and keep ascending that learning curve. You're not growing until you feel you're pushing the edges.

SELF-COACHING ACTION

Knowing that stretch assignments are among the most effective ways to learn and grow, reflect on your development needs, and make a list of such possibilities in your leadership journal. Select one that will challenge you—something that goes beyond your current level of skill and comfort. It shouldn't be something so difficult that you feel overly stressed and scared, but it needs to be something at the edges of your current capabilities. For example, if you want to improve your public-speaking abilities, you could personally stretch yourself by taking a course on public speaking or joining Toastmasters. Similarly, you could stretch yourself professionally by making a presentation at work or a national conference on something you might normally just share in written form.

Find ways to challenge yourself beyond your current capabilities. Maybe it's taking on an assignment in another country, interacting with a new customer group, or working in a functional area about which you don't know much. It could be learning to use a new computer application at work or creating a professional blog to write on issues about which you are passionate. Is there a place you could be volunteering or a task force you could join?

By the way, the learning experiences don't all need to connect directly with what you are doing right now or know today. Perhaps your growth opportunity can take the form of learning a new sport, language, or craft. It could be meeting people outside of your field or exposing yourself to movies, books, music, and places outside of your normal tastes. You could even revisit some things that you might not have liked or cared for in the past and give them a second, and possibly even new, look.

Keep coming back to this list. Challenge will always be your training ground for developing your leadership capabilities. Stretching yourself and facing new challenges isn't something to check off your list. It's something to keep doing continuously to improve and grow.

CHAPTER 11

GET CURIOUS AND GO KICK THE BALL AROUND

We've been following the inspiring life of Don Bennett for more than 30 years. Our initial encounter with Don was after he'd become the first amputee to ascend Mt. Rainier—that's 14,411 feet on one leg and two poles. We interviewed him about his leadership of the team that made that climb.[1] More recently, Don's been talking about his current passion, the Amputee Soccer League. He's working very hard to qualify amputee soccer for the Paralympic Games, and he's almost there. What's really fascinating is how it all got started.

After completing his historic climb, Don told us he was in the best shape of his life. He wanted to continue to do something to stay in good physical condition, and he started thinking about what he could do. One day Don was outside watching his son, Tom, shoot baskets. Tom kept missing, and the ball kept bouncing around. Don couldn't bend over to pick it up, so he just kicked the basketball with his one good leg. He did that several times, and later that evening he had this flash of inspiration. "Wait a minute," he remembers saying to himself. "We can ski on one leg. Why can't we play soccer with one leg?" He continued to explain:

> All I had was the inspiration. I didn't know that much about soccer. I didn't know there were even two sizes of soccer balls. . . . So the next thing is to get out and start doing something. The doing part of it is picking up a phone, calling a few friends, and saying, "Why don't you meet me over on Mercer Island. Don't bring your artificial legs. I've got an idea here. I really feel it." So when they come over, I pull out a soccer ball. They already have their crutches, and we start kicking it . . . Then things start happening. You've got to kick the ball around to get a feel for it. . . . The inspirations come with kicking the ball.

Don's amputee soccer story captures the essence of what leaders do when they are curious and have a question about something. They go kick the ball around. They experiment. They take initiative.

Research shows, for example, that the master of business administration (MBA) students who rate high on proactivity are considered by their peers as better leaders, and they engage more in extracurricular and civic activities targeted toward bringing about positive change.[2] Similarly, salespeople who score high on proactivity are likely to make more sales and receive higher commissions compared with those low on proactivity.[3] Taking initiative also results in a stronger support network and higher performance evaluations by direct supervisors.[4] Taking charge of change pays off for leaders, constituents, and their communities. Taking charge of your own development pays off in the same way.

BE CURIOUS. ASK QUESTIONS.

One simple way to exercise initiative is by being curious. When you're intrigued by something, you become inquisitive, and you're eager to know the answer to questions. That's what Don Bennett was when he asked himself, "Can people play soccer with one leg?" His curiosity and his question led him to start a movement that meaningfully occupied his time and energy for decades. The same thing can happen to you when you become curious.

It certainly happened to Brian Grazer, one of the most successful movie producers ever. Among his credits are some of the most popular films in recent years, including *Apollo 13*, *A Beautiful Mind*, *Splash*, and *Parenthood*. To what does he attribute his phenomenal success? His answer: "Curiosity has, quite literally, been the key to my success, and also the key to my happiness."[5] He also says, "Curiosity is what gives energy and insight into everything that I do. . . . For me, curiosity infuses everything that I do with a sense of possibility."[6]

How does Brian express his curiosity? "I ask questions. The questions spark interesting ideas. The questions build collaborative relationships. The questions create all kinds of connections—connections among unlikely topics, among unlikely collaborators."[7] Asking questions is one of the best ways, in his opinion, for learning from other people and expanding your own knowledge and insight into what is going on.

Brian suggests if you want to start a *curiosity conversation*, you can begin with something like this: "I've always been curious about how you ended up as a [whatever that profession is], and I was wondering if you'd be willing to spend 20 minutes talking to me about what it took to get where you are—what the key turning points in your career were?"[8] In that conversation, you can ask about a significant challenge they faced in their careers, or why they do something in a particular way, or how they handled an extraordinarily difficult situation, or how they came up with a particular idea. There is no fixed set of questions. You have to tailor them to the person and situation, but questions, sparked by curiosity and with an underlying interest in learning, always get the conversation started. Open-ended questions get people talking whereas closed-ended ones shut down conversations and unnecessarily narrow them.

Questions send people on journeys in their minds. Knowing what to ask and how to ask it are critical skills for leaders and learners. The better the question, the more rewarding the journey is. Preparing to ask questions forces you to think about what you'd like to learn. For example, do you want to improve your capacity to enlist others in a common vision? Do you want to do a better job of strengthening others? Do you want to know more about the trends that might influence the direction of your work in the next 10 years? What exactly is the journey you'd like to go on? What are the questions to which you'd like to know the answers? Whom are the best people to ask? Spending time reflecting on questions like these is vital to your development.

When you are curious about things that are outside of your regular affairs, and when you start asking questions, what you learn often becomes the catalyst for change and opens up new possibilities. This is all part of having that growth mindset that we talked about in Chapter 5. Because they believe that they are capable of always learning and developing and that their abilities aren't fixed, individuals with a growth mindset seek opportunities to learn. Gathering information about how they are doing and what they could do better is part of that process.

Which is precisely the insight that Varun Mundra, currently with Indasia Fund Advisors, gained when thinking back upon his early career experiences as a financial analyst: "When I did question the status quo—when I did come up with innovative ideas, when I followed through with the changes I suggested, got feedback, understood my mistakes, learned from them, and was open to improvements—I won the respect of the people around me. It did not matter as much whether the changes were as effective as hoped for but the fact that someone was ready to stand up and challenge what everyone else used as the norm was generally enough to get something started."

This positive view of questioning, getting feedback, and being open to improvement enabled Varun not only to initiate change, but also to earn greater trust and respect. Being curious and asking questions—even challenging ones—can lead to positive outcomes.

TRY. FAIL. LEARN. REPEAT.

When you take the initiative, when you are curious, and when you ask lots of questions, you're invariably going to come up with a long list of things to try. And it's highly likely that you're not going to know much about or how to do many of them. Good job! Leadership is not about playing it safe, and learning is not about doing what you already know how to do. Sure, you could always play only to your strengths. You may even enjoy it. But where's the growth or the opportunity for greatness in just doing that?

Leadership is always much messier in practice than it is in plans. The same goes for learning. You will stumble, make mistakes, have setbacks, and experience failures. But with a learning mindset, you can act like a scientist. Make your life a laboratory, and use it to conduct as many experiments as possible.

Try something new, fail, learn. Try something new, fail, learn. Try something new, fail, learn. This phrase should be one of your leadership mantras. Realize, as well, that you will learn that every so often you should try something entirely different, pursue another approach, or change pathways.

Charles Kettering, the founder of Delco and holder of more than 185 patents, used to say, "It doesn't matter if you try and try and try again, and fail. It does matter if you try and fail, and fail to try again." Baseball's home run champion Hank Aaron put it this way: "My motto was always to keep swinging. Whether I was in a slump or feeling badly or having trouble off the field, the only thing to do was keep swinging." And as *Harry Potter* series author J. K. Rowling said, "It is impossible to live without failing at something, unless you live so cautiously that you might as well not have lived at all, in which case you have failed by default."[9] You need to heed their lessons. History will not judge you harshly for your failures if you learn from them, but it will be unkind if you fail to try, stop swinging, or live too cautiously. Those who have left the most lasting legacies are those who have made mistakes, failed, but then tried again. That final try makes all the difference.

You can learn something about trying, failing, and trying again from how exemplary coaches help young players become successful. Consider this example from the Institute for Women's Leadership Founder and CEO Rayona Sharpnack about coaching her eight-year-old daughter's softball team. Rayona certainly knew the game: She was the first player-manager in the 1980s of the most profitable franchise of the International Women's Professional Softball League. Before that, she set a Junior Olympic record by throwing a softball 189 feet. On one of the first days of practice for her daughter's team, she had everyone try to do some batting. As she explains,

> I take a soft, spongy ball, and I toss it to the first girl.
> She's standing maybe 10 feet away, I'm throwing baby

tosses, and she screams and hides her head. So I say, "Hey, no problem, Suzy. Go to the back of the line. That's fine. Betsy, you step up." Next girl in line, she does the same thing—buries her head and screams. So I'm realizing that this is going to be a really long practice if we don't do something different.

I go out to my car where I have my handy whiteboard markers in my briefcase. I take the bag of practice balls and draw four smiley faces—red, black, blue, and green—on each ball. When you look at a ball, all you see is one smiley face. I go back out and call the girls back over: "Okay. We're going to play a different game this time," I say. "This time, your job is to name the color of the smiley face. That's all you have to do."

So little Suzy stands up, and I toss a ball by her. She watches it all the way and goes, "Red." Next girl, Betsy, gets up there. Betsy goes, "Green." They're all just chirping with excitement because they can identify the color of the smiley face, so I say, "Okay. Now I want you to do the same thing, only this time I want you to hold the bat on your shoulder when the ball goes by." Same level of success. Excitement builds. The third time through, I ask them to touch the smiley face with the bat. We beat our opponents 27 to 1 in the first game.[10]

Rayona took something that was initially frightening and gradually overcame the team's fear the girls' lack of skills. She coached the girls in increments on how to focus on the task and then to execute. That's what this example is really about: It's about getting the learners to focus on something coming at them in a way that's not frightening. For example, maybe you dread interviews. Perhaps it's the idea of having questions tossed at you that's a little scary. A simple technique is to repeat back the question and ask the questioner if you understood them correctly. This process slows the ball down, so to speak, and gives your brain a few seconds to process the question.

Whatever your developmental needs, find ways to move incrementally forward. You don't have to hit it out of the park the first time. You just have to learn something with every swing. Every time a professional baseball player goes up to bat, he believes he's going to get a hit, even though he knows that his batting average would say this is impossible. Whatever the outcome, he stores away this experience so that next time he faces that same pitcher, he's better prepared to make a hit.

Taking the initiative to learn and grow is characteristic of leaders. Nevertheless, persistence is yet another essential ingredient in the formula for successful growth and development, and we'll explore that in the next chapter.

THE KEY MESSAGE AND ACTION

The key message of this chapter is this: To challenge yourself to grow and learn, you have to take the initiative to try new things. You have to be curious. You have to ask a lot of questions. You have to experiment with new ideas and new ways of doing things. And when you initiate, question, and experiment, you are inevitably going to make mistakes and fail. The key is to learn from the experience and be willing to repeat the process. Try, fail, learn, and repeat is your mantra from this chapter.

SELF-COACHING ACTION

At the top of a page in your leadership journal, write down this statement: "When I think about what it takes to become an exemplary leader, what I am curious about is . . ." Next, record as many ideas as you can think of that respond to that statement.[11] Don't worry about the quality of the ideas—it can be as simple as "How do you lead under conditions of uncertainty?" Or, "What gives people the courage to rock the boat with their peers?" Or, "How do you let go of the negative memories connected with missing a shot or missing a deadline?" Record as many as you can think of in three minutes.

When the time is up, go back through your list, and sort the ideas into three categories regarding their importance to your learning to become the best leader you can be: very important, important, and somewhat important. Now, just focus on the items you indicated were very important, and select one of them to pursue. Then identify individuals who are likely to have some familiarity with this question and can provide you some insights from their experience. Reach out to at least one on the list within the next week to schedule a curiosity conversation with them. Follow this up with another person; or if you got that question resolved to your satisfaction, take up another issue on your list and repeat the process. Keep track of the lessons learned in your leadership journal.

CHAPTER 12

GET GRITTY AND STAY HARDY

Knowing what you want and wanting it intensely are two essential elements in the formula for success in learning, in leadership, and in life. There's yet another vital component, and that's persistence. Together these ingredients make up what University of Pennsylvania psychology professor Angela Duckworth calls *grit*.

"Grit," Angela says, "is passion and perseverance for very long-term goals. Grit is having stamina. Grit is sticking with your future, day in, day out, not just for the week, not just for the month, but also for years, and working really hard to make that future a reality. Grit is living life like it's a marathon, not a sprint."[1]

Grit is that firmness of spirit, that unyielding determination that is essential in dealing with a challenge, and it "entails working strenuously toward challenges, maintaining effort and interest over years despite failure, adversity, and plateaus in progress."[2] It is not unusual for would-be authors, or aspiring musicians, for example, to have a burst of inspiration, begin writing a chapter, or chords and lyrics, and then give up when they start to hit roadblocks or hurdles. The people who tough it out and work through those problems end up with interesting—and finished—books and songs.

Angela and her colleagues, having studied the impact of grit in a variety of settings, convincingly demonstrate that people with the most grit achieve the most positive outcomes.[3] For example, researchers have found that those who score high on grit are more likely to persist in a variety of commitments than those who score low. Grittier soldiers in training for the elite Army Special Operations Forces were more likely to complete the course, and grittier salespeople were more likely to stay in their jobs longer. Grittier high school students were more likely to graduate, and grittier men were more likely to stay married. In challenging public school settings, novice teachers in Teach for America with the most grit see greater increases in the academic gains of their students than their less gritty teacher counterparts see. In addition, spelling bee contestants who rated high on the grit scale were consistently the champions. In other words, grit is not unique to any particular domain of work; it's applicable everywhere.

Anyone who's ever tried to learn something new knows that you don't just get it in one day or two or even 10. It takes a long-term commitment. It requires dedication. It requires focus. It requires a clear and measurable goal. It requires feedback. It requires hours and hours of practice. All of that demands perseverance, not giving up in the middle, and a willingness to deal with hardship and failure. In a word, grit.

A case in point is New York Knicks forward and center Kristaps Porzingis. When the Knicks signed the 7-feet, 3-inch basketball player at 19 years of age, the fans booed. But Porzingis showed his grit. José Calderón, Knicks point guard, described his teammate this way: "He thinks about wanting to be the best. He works hard. If he has a bad game, he goes back and works hard. If he has a good game, he goes back and works hard again. He asks, he listens. He can do whatever you want with him. He's always listening to everybody. He's kind of like a sponge, getting all that information."[4] José is precisely describing grit in action.

Angela is clear, however, that because the level of dedication and commitment is so high, what you are learning has to matter to you. As she says, "People who are gritty will doggedly pursue things that they really value. It's sort of like love: You can't be in love unless there's something or someone that you're in love *with*. Similarly, employees with grit are deeply and enduringly motivated by work they find meaningful."[5] Therefore, when circumstances get tough, you are back to the questions of "Is this what I want, and how badly do I want it?"

Don Bennett, whom we mentioned in Chapter 11, didn't make it to the top of Mt. Rainier on his first attempt. He was within a few hundred feet of the summit when a severe blizzard caused him and his team to abandon the climb. Don had to prepare for another entire year before he made his successful second attempt. He didn't let that first setback deter him. Don wanted to prove to himself and other amputees that they can overcome disabilities with determination and commitment. He wanted it badly enough to keep on going.

The grit research also makes clear that there's more to becoming the best you can be than pure talent. In fact, Angela says, "Our data show very clearly that there are many talented individuals who simply do not follow through on their commitments. In fact, in our data, grit is usually unrelated or even inversely related to measures of talent."[6] In other words, just because you have a talent for something isn't a guarantee you'll become great at it. To do that, you need to get gritty.

STAY HARDY

Okay. Now you're clear about what you want. You have your purpose, you know you're passionate about it, and you're willing to persist even when times get tough. You have grit. Great.

But stuff happens. Things don't always go as planned, especially when you're trying things out for the very first time. Sometimes unwanted obstacles just come along and punch you in the gut. Sometimes outside forces derail you from your chosen course. In fact, in our research on personal-best leadership experiences, only half of the leaders we studied chose the challenges they discussed. The other half of the leaders wrote about times when the challenges found them. They talked about situations that happened unexpectedly, such as mechanical mishaps, broken supply chains, accidents, natural disasters, or projects and programs someone else, such as their immediate manager, assigned to them. Their stories also included personal tragedies, such as severe illness, injury, and death of close colleagues.

The good news is that despite these adverse circumstances, people were able to do their best even when they didn't choose to be in the situations in which they found themselves. And you can, too. Grit is an essential part of it. You need a strong work ethic and a willingness to stick with things for the long term. But you need something more to make it through these unexpected and unplanned tough times.[7] You need hardiness.

Psychologists, intrigued by people who experience a high degree of stress and yet can cope with it positively, discovered that such individuals have a distinctive attitude toward stress, which they call "psychological hardiness."[8] Hardiness is a pattern of attitudes and skills that enables people to respond adaptively under high-stress conditions. Researchers over the last 40 years have discovered that in groups as diverse as corporate managers, entrepreneurs, students, nurses, lawyers, and combat soldiers, those high in hardiness are much more likely to withstand serious challenges than those low in hardiness are.[9]

There are three fundamental beliefs to being hardy: *commitment*, *control*, and *challenge*. To turn adversity into advantage, first you need to commit yourself to what's happening. You have to get involved, engaged, and curious. You can't sit back and wait for something to happen. You also have to take control of your life. You need to make an effort to influence what is going on. Although not all your attempts may be successful, you can't sink into powerlessness or passivity. Finally, if you are going to be psychologically hardy, you need to view challenge as an opportunity to learn from both negative and positive experiences. You can't play it safe. Personal improvement and fulfillment come about as you engage in the uncertainties of life. With a hardy attitude, you can transform stressful events into positive opportunities for growth and renewal.

BOUNCE FORWARD

Together, grit and hardiness make you resilient.[10] They enable you to recover quickly from difficult circumstances. People often describe resilience as bouncing back after being knocked down by the stuff life throws at you, but from a learning perspective, it's more about bouncing forward. Instead of just returning to the state you were in before the setback occurred, you move ahead and are in better shape than you were previously.

Professional athletes are always thinking about their experience in similar situations and recalibrating what they will need to do differently the next time around—be it a sprint, another turn in the batter's box, or a penalty kick. Evidence of learning, in fact, is not making the same mistake over and over. Our research shows that the more frequently people ask, "What can we learn when things don't go as expected?" the more often they are willing to both seek out opportunities to test their skills and abilities as well as experiment and take risks, even when there is a chance of failure.

The good news is that resilience can be developed and strengthened.[11] Martin Seligman, University of Pennsylvania psychology professor and director of its Positive Psychology Center, has studied this phenomenon extensively and with some of the toughest populations—for example, active-duty soldiers in the military.[12] Marty says that in his research, "We discovered that people who don't give up have a habit of interpreting setbacks as temporary, local, and changeable."[13] People who are resilient, even in times of great stress and adversity, remain committed to moving forward by believing that what has happened isn't going to be permanent and that they can do something about the outcome.

When you experience setbacks, frustrations, disappointments, surprises, and other challenges, you may be inclined to take it personally. You may ask, "Why am I struggling?" or "Everyone else is getting it, so what's wrong with me?" As researchers have found, however, people who are the most resilient don't carry that kind of weight on their shoulders. Instead, they put the challenges into a broader context: Keep in mind that you're not the only one who's ever had these problems. Understand that others have had to deal with similar issues. Reflect on how progress in any endeavor is a result of hard work and overcoming the odds. You'll want to keep track of what worked and the lessons learned. Maintain perspective, appreciate what's been accomplished, and don't concentrate just on how much more still needs to be done.[14]

Of course, you have to acknowledge reality, but don't dwell on the threat. The setback that you just experienced while experimenting with a new behavior is an opportunity for learning. It's just feedback that what you are currently doing isn't working as well as you intended, and that's all it is. It's not a flaw in your character. It's just something you need to keep working on, and you can do that only with full, not halfhearted, commitment. You can't commit just 50 percent to becoming the best leader you can be. You commit 100 percent. There's no holding back when you want to learn to excel. Keep reminding yourself that the effort and hard work you are putting in is because what you're doing is meaningful and significant and that the future you're working toward is well worth the effort.

ACCENTUATE THE POSITIVE

Although you obviously don't control all of what is happening in the broader environment, you are still in charge of your life. When facing a new challenge, or even responding to a conflict or crisis, determine the factors you can influence and those you can't. Figure out some ways you can positively affect the outcome. For example, take a few small steps initially to get moving in the right direction and create some forward momentum. Most important, you need to place a *learning frame* around your leadership experiences.

Although there is a very real human tendency to focus on the negative, instead picture the lessons you learned and how much forward progress you made. Negativity can quickly become pervasive and contagious. It can stifle performance. Recognize the outside influences affecting the situation—many of which you had no control over—and reframe the outcome in terms of the lessons you learned. Realize that whatever mistakes you might have made, they won't likely happen again—otherwise, that would mean no learning was involved in the experience! Seriously consider how you grew as a person and as a leader from this experience, even if it meant bouncing forward. Understand what the experience taught you and how it helped prepare you for the next challenge or opportunity.

Optimism is essential in tough times. Being optimistic doesn't mean sticking your head in the sand and ignoring what's not going right. It just means that you approach unpleasantness in a more productive manner. That typically begins with your self-talk—that endless stream of unspoken thoughts that can run through your head, repeating thoughts such as "I can never be a leader" or "I should have never spoken up" or "I should never have been the first one to volunteer" and the like. This kind of negativity causes you to narrow your options and spiral downward into even more pessimistic and potentially catastrophic thinking.

Conversely, Barbara Fredrickson, professor of psychology, University of North Carolina, reports that when people experience positive emotions their minds stretch, their worldview expands, and they are open to new possibilities. They see more options and become more creative and innovative. At the same time, they are more careful in making decisions, hence more accurate, and shown to be more interpersonally effective.[15] Research also shows that people who are positive and optimistic experience significant health benefits; they live longer, have better coping skills for dealing with hardships and stress, and have lower rates of depression and cardiovascular disease.[16] To turn setbacks into advantages, you have to get involved, remain engaged, be curious, and have a positive outlook.

THE KEY MESSAGE AND ACTION

The key message of this chapter is this: Get better at leading by becoming grittier and staying hardy. You have to have a long-term purpose and pursue it with passion. You have to persist in the face of difficulties, put in the hard work, and finish what you start. It's inevitable that you will stumble, make mistakes, and experience disappointments. Everyone does. Don't let the failures stop you. These are opportunities to renew your commitment, to take charge of the change, and to see any obstacles as chances to learn. Bounce forward from the setbacks. Reaffirm your purpose. Declare what you want. Maintain your focus. Stay positive. Strengthen your resilience, and transform adversities into learning possibilities. Success comes to those who stick with it for the long haul and adapt to the ever-changing circumstances.

SELF-COACHING ACTION

How can you make sure that you are learning from your experiences and developing the grit necessary to make things happen? Set aside some time to think about a time when you suffered a severe disappointment, setback, or even failure when working toward a goal. It could have been in school, in the workplace, or in your community. It could have been years ago or very recently. With that experience in mind, make some notes in your leadership journal about your reflections on these two questions:

1. How have you reframed this experience so you could recover and move on?
2. What helped you bounce forward from it?

Take the lessons learned from this experience and apply them to the next time you face a setback. One of the key methods for developing resilience is to learn from every experience you have in life. Connecting the dots of your various experiences gives you greater clarity about the things that matter the most to you and enhances your grittiness.

CHAPTER 13

COURAGE GIVES YOU THE STRENGTH TO GROW

ourage is one of those big, bold words. It has this image of being something way out there on the edges of human experience. It's commonly associated with superhuman feats, life-and-death struggles, and overcoming impossible odds. It has such a mystique about it that you might think the concept doesn't apply to you. But looking beyond the headlines and tweets, you'll find out that this accounting of courage is certainly not the whole story. In fact, it's not even most of the story.

Courage is more prevalent than you might think. It's something every person has, and it manifests itself daily. Courage may be precious, but it is not rare. You may not access it very often, but it's there when you need it, and you'll need it if you're to become the best leader you can be. Despite all the talk about how leaders need to be courageous, very little is written for leaders about what it actually means.[1]

The ability to face adversity without being overcome by fear is courage. Like grit, it involves the capacity to persist under extremely challenging circumstances but includes the additional element of fear. Not everything that requires grit requires courage, but everything that requires courage also requires grit. Courage is not about being fear*less* so much as it is about being able to control your fear. Controlling your fear is precisely what diplomat, activist, and the longest-serving first lady of the United States, Eleanor Roosevelt, meant when she said, "You gain strength, courage, and confidence by every experience in which you really stop to look fear in the face. You are able to say to yourself, 'I have lived through this horror. I can take the next thing that comes along.' . . . You must do the thing you think you cannot do."[2]

COURAGE IS PERSONAL

Courage in the popular media gives rise to images of daring feats of bravery and nerves of steel.[3] That's the kind of big *C* courage that's part of folklore and myth. It makes for entertaining and exciting blockbuster movies. It's just not very true in everyday life. Everyday courage is more about the little *c* courage—the kind you regularly see in your organizations, communities, and homes and witnessed in personal-best leadership experiences.

Courage is mostly about ordinary encounters with life. They're not the stereotypical acts of heroism. They're not often monumental life-and-death struggles. The military and paramilitary officers we interviewed didn't tell us about being in the line of fire, nor did the businesspeople we interviewed talk about risking it all on an entrepreneurial venture. Their stories of moments of courage were much more mundane and much more personal. They were, however, almost always about making a choice to do something, rather than not.[4] For example, there were real-life cases of championing an unpopular stand on an important issue, taking initiative beyond one's previous experience levels, speaking up in public when stage fright was so powerful it made the person tremble, quitting a well-paying job to go back to school, or heading off in a new and unknown personal, professional, or spiritual direction. The outcomes were not guaranteed from such choices, and in fact, the probabilities were not very favorable. What they have in common, though, is that they are all about pursuing a noble goal or aspiration.

When you remind yourself why you are doing something challenging—when you can find the meaning in the hard work and energy required to make a change—your brain will see the situation more as a motivator than as a source of stress. Shawn Achor, chief executive officer (CEO) of Good Think Inc., where he researches and teaches about positive psychology, supports this perspective in reporting that people's brains rebel when they divorce meaning from the activity in which they are engaged.[5]

Consider how this jibes with Heather McDougall's experience in launching the Leadership exCHANGE: Global Leadership Program, which has taught and trained thousands of students from more than 80 countries. "I had no idea about how hard it was going to be to get this program off the ground, but I knew I believed in it and the impact it could have," she said. "I simply hit a point where I knew I would never give up and just found a way to move past each roadblock, and I am mighty glad I did." Heather's reflections are also consistent with what author and renowned consultant Peter Block said to us: "The truth is courage is there all the time. Fifty times a day you have to decide whether to move toward what's hard or difficult or boring or whatever, or whether to try to walk around it and take the easy way out." Maria Eitel, founding president and CEO of the Nike Foundation of Nike Inc., would agree. Courage, she says, is not about a single moment but "is a sequence of moments where you have to keep drawing from a reservoir of courage that's surrounded by a pool of fear. You have to keep tapping it and tapping it day by day, moment by moment, and not let your fear overtake you."[6]

Courage comes into play when you need to make what is for you a tough choice, but those choices are more often than not about the little things you do. Do you say yes or do you say no? Do you stay or do you leave? Do you speak or do you stay silent? None of these choices feels particularly frightening on the surface, but in the proper context they can be terrifyingly difficult. Ultimately, what takes courage, and what does not, is a very personal decision. It's not for you to decide for someone else whether something is courageous.

Margie Warrell, *Forbes* columnist, author, and founder of Global Courage, describes in her book *Stop Playing Safe* how people's brains are wired to overestimate risk, exaggerate its consequences, and underestimate their ability to handle it.[7] Fear can drive you to play safe, avoid change, and settle for less than you know is not only possible but also necessary. Just doing what you've always been doing will not move you, your team, or your organization forward. Being better requires you to have the courage to confront the current ways of thinking and try new things. Ryan Diemer, merchandise planning manager with ecommerce Quidsi, affirms what Margie has to say. "Taking risk is never easy and sometimes scary," he told us. However, he went on to observe, "Taking risks is necessary because it requires you and those you are working with to challenge not only what you are working on but how you work. Sometimes the risks pay off and sometimes they do not, but what is always true is that if you do not take a risk, you won't get any gain."

Ryan's comment also supports what Margie has to say about the remedy for fear. According to her, *action* "is the most potent antidote to fear: it breeds confidence and nurtures courage in ways nothing else can."[8] Or as theologian Mary Daly puts it, "Courage is a habit, a virtue. You get it by courageous acts. It's like learning to swim by swimming. You learn courage by couraging."[9] The reward for doing so is, at a minimum, learning—learning about yourself and learning about what might be possible. After all, you can't expect to become better at leadership, or anything else for that matter, without doing something different than you are currently doing.

IT TAKES COURAGE TO LEARN

But what's courage have to do with *learning* to become an exemplary leader?

Katherine Winkel, senior product manager, marketing, at CTI BioPharma, helps answer this question with an insight she gained when she reflected on the discussion she had with her peers about their personal-best leadership experiences:

> The similarity that most stuck out in my mind at the time, and indeed remains with me, was that in each story the person described having to overcome uncertainty and fear in order to achieve his or her best. Whatever the case, staring down uncertainty, and ultimately overcoming this hurdle, was a major theme. Typically, you would think people would describe uncertainty and fear as negative or even demotivating factors in leadership, but here it seems they are almost prerequisites for success! It has taught me that uncertainty is a necessity that drives us to do our very best.

As Katherine observed, all the personal-best stories included elements of uncertainty, and they evoked fear. Often, she noted, fear and uncertainty could reduce people's motivation and energy levels. These two conditions can cause some people to freeze, some to flee, and others to fight. In fact, some in our study initially thought that they couldn't deal with the challenge. However, in the personal-best leadership cases, people were able to call on something inside of themselves that enabled them to face the fear and do their best. That something was courage. It's interesting that when people recount their personal-best leadership experiences, they are describing moments of courage, even if they aren't consciously using that word at the time.

Positive learning experiences share common elements with the personal-best leadership experiences. And they share these same elements with moments of courage. Two of those common elements are fear and uncertainty. For example, let's say you volunteer for a stretch assignment in a foreign country where you don't speak the language, where the dominant religion is different from yours, and where the cultural norms are unfamiliar. For all the excitement that might come from such an experience—the new sights, interesting people, and growth opportunities at work—there are also fears, uncertainties, and doubts.

Or let's say you enroll in a leadership development program, and part of that experience includes 360-degree feedback. Your manager, your peers, your direct reports (if you have any), and maybe even customers are giving you feedback on your leadership practices.[10] Although you know that quality feedback is essential to improvement, this can be a very scary proposition. You don't know what people are going to say, you are concerned some might be quite negative, and you're wondering what this will do to your career and your relationships.

It takes courage to open yourself up to new information and to learn. It takes courage to expose your weaknesses to people with whom you work. It takes courage to show vulnerability, especially in public. It takes courage to admit that you're just not getting it and need help. It takes courage to take on a tough assignment and know that you might very well disappoint yourself and others in the outcomes. It takes courage to do all of these things, and yet all of them and more are a part of learning.

There's something else that personal-best leadership experiences and positive learning experiences share. They both involve something meaningful to the leader-learner. They both involve something about which you care deeply. If they didn't, you wouldn't take the risk to lead or to learn. In one research study, participants described a time they acted courageously and then were asked, "What were you trying to accomplish with this action?" Ninety-nine percent provided a clearly articulated goal. In fact, on a scale of zero to 10, the most common response to "How important was this goal to you at the time?" was 10.[11] So courage is needed when there are fear and uncertainty, but unless you care deeply about what's at stake, you're unlikely to act. Ah, you're right back to values and vision and to those brick walls that are asking, "What do you want? How badly do you want it?"

All of these elements work together. When you encounter uncertainty or adversity, it can arouse fear. In those moments, you do a quick internal check and ask yourself, "Do I care deeply about this? Is this important to me?" If you can say, "Yes, and here's why," you're going to be much more likely to take initiative to overcome your fear and push through. This process may take nanoseconds, and it may not even be a conscious decision, but something happens internally that causes you to act.

Courage gives you the energy to move forward. Courage gives you the confidence to believe you can make it. Courage gives you the strength to sustain yourself in the darkest hours. Courage makes it possible for you to raise your hand and offer an alternative, speak out and express an opinion, stand up and be counted, and step forward and move in a new direction. Courage makes it possible for you to learn to be your best.

THE KEY MESSAGE AND ACTION

The key message in this chapter is this: It takes courage to learn. When you challenge yourself to grow and develop, it's likely that you'll be doing things that scare you. When you take on stretch assignments to do things you've never done before, enroll in programs or activities to learn things you know nothing about, or put yourself into unfamiliar settings and circumstances, you are taking a risk. There will be fear and uncertainty, two elements that shape the conditions for courage, so you need to make a choice about how to move forward and find meaning and purpose in setting off in a new direction.

SELF-COACHING ACTION

Reflecting on and writing about experiences is a very powerful tool for supporting people going through stressful situations. The reflections help you see what you did in the past that you can learn from and apply to your current situation. You can realize your own capacity for courage.

In your leadership journal write about a time in your life when you believe you demonstrated courage, whatever you understand that to mean. Your story can relate to something recent or in your distant past. It can be about something that occurred at work, at school, in your community, or in any setting. In talking to people about their experiences with courage, we've found that some folks struggle with the notion that they might have acted courageously. If you have this initial response, that's pretty normal.

To get started, you might begin by completing this sentence several times until you settle on something you want to think

reflect on more deeply: "It took courage for me to _____
_____."

Then, write down your answer to this question: "In that *moment of courage* what lessons did this teach me about courage?"
You are a courageous person, so keep working on strengthening that courage muscle, and it will be ready for the unexpected fears and uncertainty you will face in becoming the best leader you can be.

PART V

FUNDAMENTAL FOUR: ENGAGE SUPPORT

You can't learn to become the best leader all by yourself. The top performers in every endeavor, including leaders, all seek out support, advice, and the counsel of others. That has a lot to do with why they turn out to be the most successful.

In learning to become an exemplary leader, you need to get connected. You need those connections to be strong and close. You need them to be personal, not just transactional. Connections open doors and give you an opportunity to observe exemplary leadership up close and in action. Often you're going to have to take the initiative to create and sustain these relationships.

You will also have to rely on the people around you to let you know the impact your actions and behaviors have on them. Their feedback is the only way that you can learn how you are doing. Getting open and honest feedback happens only when there is a foundation of mutual trust. You have to go first in creating a climate in which people trust one other enough to provide valid and useful information that will help you grow.

In the next three chapters we take a look at these key themes on becoming an exemplary leader:

- I couldn't have done it without you.
- Get connected.
- Without feedback you cannot grow.

CHAPTER 14

I COULDN'T HAVE DONE IT WITHOUT YOU

More than likely you've watched an awards show or two in your life—maybe the Primetime Emmys, the Academy Awards, the MTV Video Music Awards, the ESPY Awards, or a similar event. They are always quite theatrical, with stars parading down the red carpet, paparazzi snapping photos, and fans cheering for their favorites.

There's also a vital leadership lesson you can take away from these events.

Whenever winners come to the stage and stand at the microphone, they invariably include in their acceptance speeches comments that begin with some version of "I would like to thank," and then they list numerous people who played a role in their successes. The names might include "my mother, my father, my spouse, my manager, my agent, my coaches, my high school teacher, my cast, my crew, the other players on the team, the director, the writers, the fans"—the list goes on. Without these individuals, the award recipients wouldn't be standing there basking in the glory and the applause. And it's why they often end their remarks with "I couldn't have done it without you." For example, Paul Bonhomme, the most successful pilot in the history of the Red Bull Air Race and the only pilot to have won the World Championship three times (2009, 2010, and 2015), said: "It feels good to win the title, but it's all team work. I just fly the aeroplane, but I wouldn't be able to do that without the team I've got."[1]

The best performers in all fields know that they can't make extraordinary things happen alone. Without a cast and crew, without team members and coaches, without editors and publishers, without colleagues and customers, without fans and family, no show, no film, no athletic event, no breakthrough product, no exceptional service would ever happen. It's true for athletics and the arts, and it's true for leadership. Leadership requires collaboration, and so does learning. Although the focus of this book is on individual leaders—that would be you—you cannot do it alone. You can't lead alone, and you can't learn alone. You need to involve others to become the best leader you can be.

It's very commonplace for the best in most fields—for example, elite athletes—to express their gratitude to their coaches and to talk openly about what they learned from them. It's exceedingly rare, on the other hand, for organizational leaders to speak publicly about the help they got along the way to becoming who they are. Maybe they're embarrassed to admit they needed help. Maybe it's because they think that if they are in leadership roles, they are supposed to know it all, so they can't appear to have needed help. Maybe it's because they fear that if they admit to needing help, they'll give the impression they're somehow ignorant, inadequate, even weak. Maybe it's because they're worried that people will question their competence. Maybe it's because they fear the possibility of rejection, that they'll be a burden, or somehow indebted to others. Maybe it's because it's not acceptable in some cultures to admit that you don't know how to do something.[2]

Whatever the reason, organizational leaders typically don't mention, let alone brag about, the coaching and support that helped them learn, grow, and achieve. It's a shame, really, because it would make leaders both more human and more likeable if they were to acknowledge that without the advice and support of others, they would be unable to excel. It would also set a very good example for aspiring leaders. They need role models who acknowledge how important social support is to success at any level and in every endeavor. One further benefit: Gratitude, it turns out, is the best predictor of personal well-being.[3]

ASK FOR HELP AND SUPPORT

The news media, novels, and movies often portray leadership as an act of rugged individualism—of one daring person who charges out into the wilderness all alone to take on a challenge, create something new, and change the world. Well, the challenge part is true enough, but not the alone part. When people told us about their personal-best leadership experiences, they repeatedly echoed what Eric Pan, regional head, Chartered Institute of Management Accountants (South China), told us: "No matter how capable you are as a leader, you won't be able to deliver results all by yourself." Likewise, IBM's senior development manager, Amit Tolmare, explained: "No leader has ever been successful marching alone. You need to count on the teamwork and collaboration of people around you." Making something extraordinary happen has always required the engagement, trust, and support of others; and similarly, you can't learn to lead in a vacuum. Without the trust, support, and encouragement of others, you will not be able to venture out very far.

To become the best at leading, or at anything, you have to challenge yourself, take on stretch assignments, step outside your comfort zone, experiment with new ways of doing things, make mistakes, and learn from failure. These are all just a natural part of the process when you're learning to become the best leader you can be. That's all well and good; however, you're not likely to do these things if there's no one there to teach you, coach you on how to improve, cheer you on and cheer you up, catch you when you fall, and comfort you when you hit the wall. Learning to lead requires getting help from others. Social support is a necessary condition for growth and development, particularly when that learning is challenging. "The single most important thing you can do to help ensure your future success," according to the Gallup organization's study of more than 27 million employees worldwide, is to find someone who has an interest in your development.[4]

For example, Benjamin Bloom, professor of education at the University of Chicago, and his colleagues investigated the development of talent in 120 elite performers—individuals who had won international competitions or awards in their respective fields. The study included concert pianists, sculptors, research mathematicians, research neurologists, Olympic swimmers, and tennis champions. Their research "provided strong evidence that no matter what the initial characteristics (or gifts) of the individuals, unless there is a long and intensive process of encouragement, nurturance, education, and training, the individuals will not attain extreme levels of capability in these particular fields."[5] Further to the point about social support, they concluded that no one ever reached the top in any endeavor on his or her own. The active support of families and teachers, for example, was crucial at every step along the journey. It's worth noting that these were the elite performers in their respective fields, and every single one of them needed help.

None of this means that you are doomed to mediocrity if you weren't raised in a family that provided early childhood support for you to learn to lead. What it does mean, however, is that whenever you begin learning leadership—or any new set of skills—you need to be able to count on others to help you become the best you can be. If it's not there for you, you need to take the initiative to find it because research across a broad range of disciplines consistently demonstrates that social support enhances learning, productivity, psychological well-being, and even physical health. In fact, George Vaillant, Harvard professor of psychiatry, who directed the world's longest continuous study of physical and mental health, said, "The only thing that really matters in life are your relationships to other people."[6]

SEEK ADVICE

Consider what researchers found when analyzing the speeches of baseball players when inducted into the National Baseball Hall of Fame. As elite athletes, these players had achieved the highest recognition in a field demanding top physical skills. But for almost two-thirds of the recipients, their words of appreciation were less about the technical or practical assistance they received and more about emotional support and friendship. Players elected in their very first year of eligibility mentioned social support even more prominently.[7] No one gets to the top of any endeavor alone. Every recent member of *Fortune* magazine's 40 Under 40 leaders, for example, said that he or she relied on the counsel of a broad group of advisors along the way, "whether investors, mentors, college professors, board members, or yes, Mom and Dad."[8]

Of course, you have to find a balance between trying to learn something on your own and sucking it up, swallowing your pride, and admitting that you are stuck and need help. One recent college graduate said to us, "My boss, on the one hand, expects me to figure out things for myself and not come running to her for help all the time. On the other hand, she also expects me not to torture myself for hours and days when I can just come to her for help and advice."

When seeking help from others, the point is not to get someone else to do your work. The point is to get help to learn. Be prepared to describe what you've already tried and what you've learned. Come armed with a few action possibilities of your own so that it doesn't appear that you're asking for a handout. But when you're stuck, don't delay asking for help for too long. Often, the longer you wait, the worse problems can become, and the more limited the options are.

Don't assume you know what others know, and don't discount their willingness to help. Until you ask, you can't be sure of either. Researchers have found that people minimize the probability of someone helping them out when asked. Across a range of requests occurring in both experimental and natural field settings, people underestimated by as much as 50 percent the likelihood that someone else would agree to a direct request for help.[9] For example, you might predict that you'll have to ask 20 people to get the help you need, and in actuality, it will be less than half that many. Most people are happy to help. They feel complimented that you recognize their experience and competence.

Finally, don't worry about other people thinking less of you if you seek advice. In fact, just the opposite is true. "Contrary to conventional wisdom and lay beliefs," report researchers, "we find that asking for advice *increases* perceptions of competence."[10] As long as the task is difficult, you make the request personally, and you ask for advice from someone who's competent in the area, your request for advice strengthens the perception that you know what you are doing. Reaching out to others for advice on tough challenges on which you need help not only builds your competence but also increases the sense in others that they can have confidence in your leadership.

EMPATHY IS ESSENTIAL

Your capacity to be empathic goes a long way in your ability to garner assistance and support from other people. Indeed, empathy is among the most human of all abilities, playing a profound role in being able to make meaningful connections and building quality relationships. Understanding and sharing the feelings of others enables you to interpret people's viewpoints effectively. Professor Ernest J. Wilson III, dean of the Annenberg School for Communication and Journalism at the University of Southern California, asserts that empathy is the most essential attribute leaders need to succeed in today's volatile, uncertain, complex, and ambiguous (VUCA) world.[11]

Recent research underscores just how valuable this is now and will be in the future. Harvard professor David Deming found that since 1980, the labor market's growth in jobs requiring social skills outpaced the growth in jobs requiring routine skills, even routine analytical skills. Equally important, the jobs requiring good social skills are higher paying than those that don't require them. Although jobs requiring both high cognitive and high social skills are at the top of the earnings list, jobs requiring high cognitive skills but low social skills pay less than those requiring high social skills. Geoff Colvin reinforces this finding in his book *Humans Are Underrated* when he explains, "The most valuable people are increasingly relationship people."[12]

Empathy is more than the Golden Rule of doing unto others what you would have done unto you. Why? Because other people often have different tastes and preferences than your own; and this is especially true when you're working in a multicultural environment. Empathetic people have an insatiable interest in others, and they remain open to and excited about learning from others' experiences and perspectives, however different from their own these may be.

To enrich the kind of support and help you get, demonstrate your empathy by reaching out to others who are not exactly like you and listening attentively to what they have experienced. Find opportunities to step outside the comfort of your own experiences. For example, interact with people who have different political views from your own, discover what life is like for those living on the margins, find out what it means to affiliate with a religion other than your own, or engage with those whose work or organizations make assumptions at variance with your own. Consider Gandhi's declaration during the conflicts between Muslims and Hindus before India's independence in 1947: "I am a Muslim, and a Hindu, and a Christian, and a Jew, and so are all of you." Highly empathic people challenge their own preconceptions and prejudices by searching for what they share with others rather than what divides them and by gaining firsthand experiences with how other people live and work.

Not surprisingly, empathy and learning are positively related. Your ability to understand others, walk in their shoes, adopt their perspectives, and be open-minded and nonjudgmental about others' experiences improves critical-thinking skills. It also fosters insight, discourages hasty problem identification, discourages rigidity, encourages flexibility, and reduces stress. All of these benefits are welcome in any setting, but empathy becomes an even more valuable skill as the workplace becomes more global.

THE KEY MESSAGE AND ACTION

The key message of this chapter is this: You can't learn to become the best leader you can be without the help and support of others. The top performers in every endeavor all have coaches and trainers. The same is true of the best leaders. The support, advice, and counsel of experts have a direct bearing on your learning to become an exemplary leader. You sustain and strengthen those connections through being empathetic.

SELF-COACHING ACTION

In Chapter 10, you reflected on your development needs, made a list of possibilities that would stretch you, and found ways to challenge yourself beyond your current capabilities. Now, who can help you with these?

In your leadership journal jot down a list of all the people who assist you in your growth. They could be from your workplace, home, or community. Think of people who could offer you support, training, and guidance, as well as those who could challenge you to move outside of your comfort zone. Think of them as your learning and development team. Whom do you want on that team? What roles will each play? What specific help do you need from each? For instance, some might be role models, others might be coaches, and others might be simply encouragers. Offer to buy them each a cup of coffee or tea, sit down, and have a chat. Let them know the support you need and how they can help. Moreover, don't be shy about your requests. More often than not people will be glad to share their knowledge and experience if asked.

CHAPTER 15

GET CONNECTED

How did you learn to lead? We've asked this question of everyone in our research on Personal-Best Leadership Experiences. No matter where people are in their careers, or how they acquired their leadership knowledge and skills, the answer comes down to two key categories.

The first is trial and error. There's no substitute for learning by doing, especially doing things that challenge you. Typical comments are ones like this from Denise Straka, vice president of corporate insurance for Calpine Corporation: "One of the ways I learned to lead was by trial and error and then acknowledging mistakes and doing things differently next time."[1] Whether it's taking on a new supervisory role, leading a team project, heading up a volunteer community improvement effort, chairing a professional association's annual conference, captaining a sports team, or starting up a business venture, the more chances you have to serve in a leadership role, the more likely it is you'll develop the skills to lead. You just get in there and try things. Some stuff works and other stuff doesn't; but when you step back and reflect on what happened, these experiences yield valuable lessons on leadership.

The second most frequently mentioned way in which individuals learn to lead is from *people*. Not only do you need other people's support, as we noted in the previous chapter, but you also need to discover the lessons experienced leaders can teach you. You don't have to engage in all the experiences yourself; you can learn by observing how other people lead, both well and poorly. Cliff Dennett, executive vice president and senior lending officer, Pinnacle Bank, echoes this message in telling us that he's "been fortunate to work and be mentored by several excellent leaders, and over the years I've made mental notes of the positive attributes these leaders exhibit." Look around. There are people who can show you what leadership looks like in the real world.[2]

Experienced leaders are not only role models. They are also necessary connections to information, resources, and, of course, other people. They make it a lot easier for you to get doors to open, and they increase the chances you'll get to meet those who can provide exceptional learning and career opportunities in your future.

To become an exemplary leader, you have to connect to others. You have to invite people into your life. You have to knock on doors and introduce yourself. You have to be curious and want to interact with them. You have to be willing to get close to people and open up with them. You need to plug into the resources others have, find opportunities to observe leaders in action, and learn the social skills that will facilitate social interaction. You don't have to be a fiery extrovert to do all this; you can be a quiet introvert and still make lots of connections.[3] Whichever you are, you have to network and make connections, building relationships with people.

MAKE SOCIAL CONNECTIONS

When it comes to making connections, you need to be the first mover. You need to take the initiative. Go knock on doors or call people up, and ask them whether they'd spend a few minutes with you talking about their work. Brian Grazer, the movie producer mentioned in an earlier chapter, is extraordinary at this.

"I had a rule for myself," Brian explained. "I had to meet one new person in the entertainment business every day." Initially his conversations were just with entertainment business insiders, but "pretty quickly I realized that I could actually reach out and talk to anyone, in any business that I was curious about. It's not just showbiz people who are willing to talk about themselves and their work—everyone is."[4] Brian estimates that these conversations number more than 500, and they've led to movies, business ventures, and creative endeavors. Most important, they've enriched him with a wealth of knowledge and information that he can draw upon every day of his life.

The evidence around social capital strongly supports Brian's belief about the importance of relationships.[5] Humans are social animals and hardwired to connect.[6] Survival and growth depend on it. The information economy wouldn't exist unless people needed to connect. Information flows depend on social networks, and through norms of reciprocity they mutually benefit everyone involved. People will do extraordinary things for one another, and you need to both build and tap into this urge to form social networks. The more connections and relationships you have, the more access you'll have to richer and more diverse sources of information and knowledge; they enlarge the potential pool of people from whom you can learn and seek guidance. James Citrin, a senior partner and member of the board of the search firm Spencer Stuart and the author of *The*

Career Playbook: Essential Advice for Today's Aspiring Young Professional, explains that relationships are "critical both to getting jobs and being successful on the job, as well as being one of the most essential factors to overall happiness."[7] Research shows very clearly that when social connections are numerous and strong, there's more trust, reciprocity, information flow, collective action, happiness, and wealth.

It's important to recognize and appreciate that no one gave Brian the work assignment to have curiosity conversations. He came up with that idea all on his own. And he did it when he was fresh out of college. You can do the same thing. You can make a rule for yourself to have a curiosity conversation with one person each day. If it can't be once a day, make it once a week. Get curious and get more connections.

QUALITY CONNECTIONS MATTER

As you advance in your career, the *quality* of your connections becomes more and more significant. Recent longitudinal research has found that when people are in their twenties, the number of social interactions predicts greater well-being. As people move into their thirties and beyond, however, the quality of relationships becomes more important.[8] Your ability to cultivate intimacy with others increasingly becomes a significant factor in your personal and professional development.

Researchers have shown that "high-quality connections contribute to individual flourishing and to team and organizational effectiveness."[9] People who have high-quality connections are healthier, have higher cognitive functioning, are broader thinkers, are more resilient, are more committed to the organization, and know better whom to trust and not to trust. They also exhibit more learning behaviors. With high-quality relationships, people are more open, which means they more readily and fully understand themselves and the viewpoints of others. Greater quality in your connections results in more attentiveness to what's going on around you and how to approach various activities. The quality of your relationships significantly influences the quality of your learning.

You still have to be you, but you can more effectively develop your leadership abilities by connecting to people who, based on their experiences, can teach you about the things you would like to achieve and the skills you'd like to acquire. Find out about their struggles, hardships, and mistakes as well as their accomplishments. Consider connecting with people who are not particularly well known or flashy but who exhibit deep competence, unswerving dedication, and a good sense of who they are. Most important, choose people who make you feel good about yourself because the purpose of this relationship, after all, is to encourage and inspire you to improve yourself. The people with whom you connect should be people who care about you and are interested in your betterment.

In finding and selecting people with whom to connect, start by thinking local. Who is a friend or colleague at work who's been successful at leading in the context in which you're interested? Who has mastered a leadership skill you would most like to learn? Who exercises excellent judgment, is insightful, or is visionary? Who is someone you know who has overcome rejection or obstacles in the course of a career? Think of what you most need right now, and then look nearby for people you know. Start locally and then expand that circle out as you gain more experience in engaging with others around your learning agenda. Travis Carrigan, a senior engineer at Pointwise Inc., tells us that he's been doing this for the last few years, and he says that it's led to some great projects and collaborative work. "These relationships," he says, "are phenomenal at helping me become a better leader, listener, and engineer."

LOOK FOR POSITIVE ROLE MODELS

People become the leaders they observe. If you want to become an exemplary leader, you have to watch and study exemplary leaders. "Modeling is the first step in developing competencies," says Stanford professor Albert Bandura, one of the world's leading authorities on the topic. "By observing modeled performances, individuals gain knowledge about the dynamic structure of the skill being acquired. Repeated opportunities to observe the modeled activities enable observers to discover the essential features of that skill, organize and verify what they know, and give special attention to missing aspects."

To become the best leader, you'll need more than the knowledge, skills, and attitudes that make you a successful leader; you also must understand how to apply these across a variety of real-life settings. Although reading stories and biographies of leaders is helpful, as is watching videos and movies, it's a lot more useful to observe and engage in real time with real people who have mastered leadership competencies.

If you want to improve your ability to give an inspiring presentation, watch and study someone who's mastered that skill. If you want to know how to handle a difficult negotiation, find a way to observe one in action. If you want to know how to become more future oriented, spend time with someone who's mastered that art and science. You can't know how to do something until you've seen it done successfully. Observing models of mastery is an extraordinarily effective development methodology.

Of course, you will eventually have to do this on your own. You won't be able to pull out your tablet every time you are about to perform a task and watch an expert do it first. However, it helps enormously when you can start learning from a good role model and then create a mental picture of performing that same skill yourself. For example, we asked Taylor Bodman, general partner at Brown Brothers Harriman, to reflect on the leadership role models in his life. He was able to tell us in great detail why he selected each person, what each did, how he felt about each, and what he learned from each that enabled him to be a better leader. All of them were people he knew personally and not the people who make the covers of magazines or the nightly news.

Taylor's experience is consistent with our research showing that the majority of people find their role models close to home. Although it's commonplace in the popular press to talk about the rich and famous, that is not where most people find exemplars from whom they learn about leadership. After asking people for nearly 30 years to recall who has been their most important leader role model, the results are consistent over time. For people younger than 30 years of age, the top three categories of leader role models are family member, teacher or coach, and community or religious leader. For individuals older than 30, the top three categories are family member, business leader (usually an early-career supervisor), and then teacher or coach.

Positive role models are also necessary because it is impossible to excel based upon a negative. You can excel only to a positive example. You can know 100 things not to do, but if you don't know even one thing to do, then you can't perform the task. Likewise, what you can learn from an ineffective supervisor is quite limited; knowing what you don't want to emulate is a poor substitute for knowing what you do want to imitate. It's essential to have positive role models in your life because they are the individuals who can demonstrate the most skillful execution of a leadership behavior or practice.

Obviously, no two people will have the same set of role models. Moreover, your role models don't need to be exemplary at every leadership behavior; that would be a tall order to fill. Focus on one or two skills you most want to learn, and look for an individual who's good at those. Your role models can come from anywhere (home, work, or community), so look around. You'll greatly benefit from watching them work.

THE KEY MESSAGE AND ACTION

The key message of this chapter is this: To learn to become an effective leader, you need to get connected. You need good advice and counsel, and you need people who can open doors for you. Identify who those people are, how you can reach out to them, and what you can do to improve the quality of your relationships with them. You're going to have to take the initiative to create and sustain relationships. Find people who are role models; observe how they do what they do. Follow their example.

SELF-COACHING ACTION

In the last chapter, we asked you to surround yourself with individuals who could provide you support and encouragement. Now we would like you to go one step further and propose that you put together a personal board of directors. Your personal board should have four to seven people whom you respect and trust and to whom you can turn when you need counsel on tough questions and ethical dilemmas, guidance during transitions, advice about personal development needs, and help in staying true to your values and beliefs. They should represent a diverse set of skills and experiences and be role models of many of the skills you'd like to develop.[10]

Whom would you like to be on your personal board of directors? Make a list in your leadership journal of their names and, ideally, what help you'd like from each person. Start by asking one person to be on your board. Tell that person what you're up to, and ask whether they'd be available for a cup of coffee every so often to offer advice and counsel. You can then go out and find a second board member.

CHAPTER 16

WITHOUT FEEDBACK YOU CANNOT GROW

G arrison Keillor, author and host of the radio variety program *A Prairie Home Companion*, closes the news portion of every show with the line "Well, that's the news from Lake Wobegon, where all the women are strong, all the men are good-looking, and all the children are above average." Although it's supposed to be in Minnesota, this fictional town with its illusion of superiority could be anywhere. That's because time and time again people respond to surveys indicating that they are *above average* regardless of the skill and competence examined.[1] For example, more than 90 percent of university professors rate themselves above average in teaching ability, and more than two-thirds believe they are among the top 25 percent.[2] Nearly two-thirds of American drivers rate themselves as excellent or very good.[3] Most people think they are fairer than their peers are.[4] All of these are, of course, mathematically impossible. Moreover, studies show a fairly low correlation between people's self-evaluations and objective assessments of their work-related skills.[5]

Favorable self-perceptions may be good for self-esteem, but they aren't very useful when it comes to improving skills and abilities in teaching, driving, leading, or anything else. The reality is that no one is as good as he or she thinks or as bad as he or she may believe either. Before you can engage in serious self-improvement, you need an accurate assessment based on a set of reliable standards. The best cure for this Lake Wobegon effect is feedback.

Valid and useful feedback is essential to learning. Learning cannot happen without knowing how you are doing and without identifying what you need to change to improve. Our research clearly shows that the best leaders are active learners, never believing that they know it all.[6] They remain open to new ideas from a variety of sources, and when it comes to leadership, that feedback has to come from the people you are attempting to influence. They're the only ones who can reliably tell you the impact your actions have on them. Although you have to prepare yourself for those who never have anything positive to say as well as for those who are only going to sugarcoat their comments, asking for feedback is a habit you need to develop.

The problem is that most people don't want feedback, don't ask for feedback, and don't get much of it unless it's forced on them.[7] For instance, how often do you ask for feedback on how your actions affect other people's performance? Data from well over 2.5 million individuals reveals that this particular behavior ranks last among all 30 leadership behaviors on the *Leadership Practices Inventory.*[8] Not only do people self-report that this is the leadership behavior in which they engage least frequently, but their managers, colleagues, and direct reports also rank it as least frequently demonstrated by the leader.[9]

Everyone agrees on this point. Asking for feedback is not something very many leaders are inclined to do.

FEEDBACK MAKES YOU VULNERABLE

Why is it that feedback is so often treated like an unwanted guest at a party? Why do most people shy away from something that has so many personal, professional, and organizational benefits? A major reason people, and especially those in leadership positions, aren't proactive in asking for feedback is they are afraid of feeling exposed—exposed as not being perfect, as not knowing everything, as not being as good at leadership as they should be, and as not being up to the task.

Douglas Stone and Sheila Heen, authors of *Thanks for the Feedback: The Science and Art of Receiving Feedback Well*, report that the feedback process strikes at the tension between two fundamental human needs—the need to learn and grow and the need to be accepted just the way you are.[10] Consequently, even what seems like a mild, gentle, or relatively harmless suggestion can leave a person feeling angry, anxious, unfairly treated, or profoundly threatened.

Feedback is most often viewed through the frames of evaluation and judgment: good or bad, right or wrong, top 10 percent or bottom quartile. These frames raise resistance, not just on the receiving end, but also on the sending end. Management consultants Jack Zenger and Joseph Folkman have reported that while people believe constructive criticism is essential to their career development, people frequently don't feel comfortable offering it. They also report that those individuals who are most uncomfortable giving negative feedback are also significantly less interested, in turn, in receiving it from others.[11]

Learning to become a better leader requires feedback because it is essential for learning and growth. How do you get more comfortable giving and receiving feedback? The first thing you have to do is view feedback through the frame of a growth mindset instead of a fixed mindset, which we talked about in Chapter 5.

With a growth mindset, feedback becomes information that is an integral part of learning. You say to yourself and others, "This is valid and useful information that will help me become better at leading." When you frame it that way, it becomes less about your deficiencies and more about your opportunities. This is exactly how Ed Beattie, general manager at Chorus, New Zealand's largest telecommunications infrastructure company, looks at feedback. "There is no feedback that Ed won't listen to seriously," according to one of his direct reports. "He doesn't want us to hold anything back, even and especially feedback about his personal performance. He wants to know what's going on—the good, the bad, and the ugly. Everyone has the ability to approach him openly and candidly without fear of him getting angry or defensive."

With a growth mindset, as Ed illustrates, you make different assumptions about both the feedback and yourself. You assume that you can learn from criticism, that your capabilities are always evolving, that you can overcome obstacles and deficiencies if you put in the effort, and that even the most painful information can motivate you to improve.[12] This may initially be difficult to do, but if you practice reframing feedback as an opportunity to get better at what you do, then it'll get easier over time. Of course, not all feedback you receive will be negative. You also want to know what you're doing well so that you can build on your strengths.

In addition, you have to send an affirming message to those from whom you'd like feedback. You have to let them know that you see it as essential to your growth and development, that you value their input, and that you appreciate their willingness to share their observations and perceptions with you. You have to demonstrate that you've heard and understood their feedback, not only in your words but also in your subsequent behaviors. Most important, no one should ever be punished for accepting the invitation to give you a candid and direct assessment of your actions as a leader.

Learning to be a better leader requires considerable self-awareness, and it requires making yourself vulnerable by opening yourself up to information that may not always make you comfortable or happy. Still, there is simply no denying that you can't get better without sufficient feedback about how well you are doing right now. An essential part of that process is making sure that you base your relationships on a firm foundation of trust.

FEEDBACK REQUIRES TRUST

Because you don't know what people are going to say when you ask them for feedback, most likely you're going to seek feedback from people you trust. The same goes for others. They are much more likely to be open and honest with you if they trust you. It's a reciprocal process. You have to trust them, and they have to trust you. So, if you're going to put asking for feedback on your schedule, you're also going to have to put trust building on your agenda.

Trust is all about openness, and trust building involves creating an environment in which people can be open and honest with each other. You'll need to set the stage for this by showing others you value and respect their opinions and perspectives. That means listening to them. That means moving outside of your comfort zone and letting go of always doing it your way or even the way it's always been done before. Building trust means not making commitments you can't keep. It requires not overpromising regardless of how much you wish you could do something. Building trust requires a willingness to believe in the goodwill and intentions of others. It also means that on those occasions when someone lets you down and disappoints you, you exercise the grace to let him or her know that everyone is human and makes mistakes.

Trust is relying on others and having confidence in them, and this can be difficult enough for anyone, but especially for leaders. Trusting others as a leader typically puts your credibility and career on the line. You're exposed to the consequences of others' actions, not just to those of your own. That's the risk leaders accept for the possibility of accomplishing something that has never been done before. As Jonathan Moss, chief executive officer (CEO) at Frucor Australia explained, "Trust is ultimately about opening yourself up to others, making yourself vulnerable."

Learning to be the best leader you can be means building trusting relationships. It means building the kinds of relationships in which all parties feel safe enough to risk being open and honest with each other. You won't get the kind of feedback you need until those conditions are met. When you think about it, trust has always been an important part of the best learning environments. Whether it's between a student and a teacher, a parent and a child, a coach and a player, or a manager and a direct report, trust is a huge factor in determining whether learning will occur.

In the game of trust, leaders have to ante up first. Your constituents are waiting for you to make the first move.

YOU HAVE TO GO FIRST

It's highly unlikely that your colleagues, direct reports, manager, or even friends are going to knock on your door and say, "I'd like to give you some feedback." Few people, if any, will voluntarily approach you with their direct assessment of how your actions are affecting them. The only way to break this cycle is for you to go first. That's what leaders do, anyway. Go first. If you want genuine feedback about how you're doing, you're going to have to be the first to ask for it.

Going first was exactly the approach taken by Steve Hamilton,[13] vice president at a Midwestern financial services company. Steve knew that direct personal feedback was invaluable to his own as well as others' growth and development, so he asked his team members to give him a 360-degree performance review. This had never been done before in the organization. Knowing that it would be difficult for people to speak openly about his performance while he was present, after a brief orientation explaining the process, he left his team to evaluate his performance in private. They were reluctant and somewhat unsure about how to proceed, and whether they could trust Steve, as well as keep confidences among themselves. The team worked through these issues, and at Steve's request, they delivered their feedback to him face-to-face.

"The feedback that I received was kind of hard to hear," Steve later told us, but then he added: "And that was really one of the benefits to the group. To take that personal risk—to model for the group that it's okay to place yourself at personal risk and take that honest feedback. What I hope the team members would come away with was a sense that it's okay to be in that environment, that feedback is necessary for growth, and then to see how you accept that feedback and what you do with it."

By going first and asking for help from others, Steve opened himself up to new information and accepted the risk that not everything he would hear would necessarily be positive. However, by making himself vulnerable in this way, he built trust with this team. Because of his ability to ask others for help, his team gained a newfound respect for the feedback process—and they subsequently were more willing to ask for feedback from Steve and one another.

The late John Gardner, leadership scholar and presidential adviser, once remarked, "Pity the leader caught between unloving critics and uncritical lovers."[14] No one likes to hear the constant screeching of harpies who have only nasty things to say. At the same time, no one ever benefits from, nor believes, the sycophants whose flattery aims at gaining favor. To stay honest with yourself, you need *loving critics*—people who care about you and want you to do well; and because they care about your well-being, they are willing to give you the sort of feedback you need to become the best leader you can be.

THE KEY MESSAGE AND ACTION

The key message of this chapter is this: If you are going to grow and develop your leadership skills, you will have to rely on people around you to let you know about the impact of your behaviors and actions. Their feedback is the only way you can learn how you make others feel and the extent to which you have a positive, neutral, or negative impact on their performance and engagement. Getting open and honest feedback can happen only when there is a foundation of mutual trust. As a leader, you have to go first in creating a climate in which people trust one other enough to provide valid and useful information that will help you grow.

SELF-COACHING ACTION

Before your next team meeting, take one of the people you trust aside and tell that person that you'd like feedback on how your behaviors are impacting the discussion and decisions and that you'd like to have a conversation about this after the meeting. Say you'd like observations on these two questions: "In the meeting what am I doing that favorably contributes to the discussion and invites others into the conversation? What am I doing that gets in the way of folks being heard, building upon the comments of others, and making decisions with maximum buy-in and accountability?" There are other kinds of questions you can ask, but the point is that you want someone to play the role of a coach whose job it is to look for what you're doing well and what you need to improve. Make sure to record the feedback in your leadership journal. Over time, you'll be able to track your progress.

The first time you do this, make sure you select a person with whom you have a good relationship. That will make it easier both for him or her to provide feedback and for you to be open to what he or she has to share. You could even solicit such feedback from a different person at each meeting. This way others might be encouraged to follow your example—to everyone's benefit.

And when you've gotten the feedback you've asked for, all you ever need to say is "Thank you." There's no need for you to defend or justify your behavior. Just listen with care and respect for that person's perspective. "Thank you" is a time-honored and proper way to express your appreciation for any gift you've received.

PART VI

FUNDAMENTAL FIVE: PRACTICE DELIBERATELY

You can't get any better at leading without practice. Moreover, the time spent practicing won't amount to much unless you adhere to some discipline. Knowing your strengths and building upon them is important, but so is realizing that you are weak in some areas and addressing them.

Context significantly affects your ability to grow and thrive as a leader. Environments of trust and respect are critical, as are opportunities for learning, support for risk, and role models from whom you can learn. Sometimes you'll have the good fortune to work in those environments, and other times you'll have to take charge of creating your own culture of leadership.

Being an exemplary leader requires a lifelong, daily commitment to learning. No matter how many summits you've ascended, you have to take a step every day to improve—one reflection at a time, one question at a time, and one lesson at a time. You have to commit to the habit of learning something new every day and the habit of assessing your progress every day.

In the next three chapters we take a look at these key themes on becoming an exemplary leader:

- Leadership takes practice, and practice takes time.
- Context matters.
- Learning leadership must be a daily habit.

CHAPTER 17

LEADERSHIP TAKES PRACTICE, AND PRACTICE TAKES TIME

G lenn Michibata, a three-time all-American who played professional tennis for 10 years, spent 12 years as head coach of men's tennis at Princeton. When we asked him how much time his players had to practice every day, Glenn's response was "I tell them they need to practice two hours every day if they want to stay the same, more if they want to get better."

Glenn's experience taught him that becoming the best player took more than a brief daily workout, more than a weekly tune-up, more than a monthly coaching session, and more than an annual weekend retreat. Similarly, here's what Lang Lang, the 33-year-old Chinese concert pianist, said when we asked him about his practice routine: "I practiced 8 hours a day for the first 15 years." And, now? "Three hours," he said, "each and every day." Researchers studying some of the most talented people in history have found that not a single individual produced incredible work without putting in many years of practice.[1]

Raw talent alone is not sufficient to achieve greatness. It takes practice; but just not any kind of practice works, however, say researchers who have studied top performance across a wide variety of domains, such as surgery, acting, chess, writing, computer programming, ballet, music, aviation, and firefighting. They report, "To people who have never reached a national or international level of competition, it may appear that excellence is simply the result of practicing daily for years or even decades. However, living in a cave does not make you a geologist. Not all practice makes perfect. You need a particular kind of practice—*deliberate practice*—to develop expertise."[2]

Just because people have the title of manager doesn't make them leaders, and it doesn't mean they are skillful at leading. Too often, people promoted into managerial positions are good at technical or process matters, working with things, but not particularly comfortable with, skillful in, or even interested in leadership and working closely with people. Similarly, too often people engage in an activity and just assume that they will continue to get better at it over time just because they do it often.

Deep learning just doesn't happen without intentionality and intensity. It takes a lot more than experiencing something to become the best at it. For example, you learned to drive a car, and most likely you've driven tens of thousands of miles. And, also most likely you stopped years ago doing anything intentional to become a better driver, let alone training to become the best driver you can be—for instance, attending the Porsche Sport Driving School in Atlanta, Georgia.

Ask comedian Steve Martin about his rise in comedy and his advice for aspiring performers. His answer is not about how to write jokes or how to find a good agent; he recommends, "Be so good they can't ignore you."[3] It takes lots of hard work, practicing and polishing your craft to get that good. The same goes for leadership. Mastering leadership takes a lot more than showing up. It takes hours of deliberate practice over lots of years.

PRACTICE, PRACTICE, PRACTICE

And just what does it mean to practice *deliberately?*

To begin with, you will not engage in just any activity. Instead, you will engage in one designed specifically to improve performance. For example, going to the driving range and hitting a bucket of balls is not deliberate practice, especially when you do this just before playing a round. It's more like warming up. It may be fun, and you may get a bit better, but it's not the route to becoming the best. The key word here is *designed*, meaning there is a methodology, and there is a very specific goal. More often than not, you work with an instructor, coach, or teacher to select the goal and the method. Similarly, just visualizing what you would like to happen is very unlikely to get you there. Says University of Calgary Professor Piers Steel, in his book *The Procrastination Equation*, "The only wealth created by creative visualization is a rich fantasy life."[4]

Second, practice is not a onetime event. Engaging in a designed learning experience just once or twice doesn't cut it. It has to be done over and over and over again until it's automatic. That takes hours of repetition. There's no hard-and-fast rule about the number of hours needed. The time required needs to fit with the skill you're practicing. Moreover, during repetition you need to pay as much attention to the methodology as to the goal. CrossFit training in the gym, working out with weights, with specified repetitions and varied fitness stations, is a whole lot different from running around your neighborhood while talking with a friend on your mobile. Sloppy execution is not acceptable to top performers.

Another important characteristic of deliberate practice is the availability of feedback. Without knowing how you are doing, it's difficult to gauge whether you're getting close to your goal and whether you're executing correctly. Although there may come a time when you're accomplished enough to assess your performance, you need a coach, mentor, or some other third party to help analyze how you did. And that person needs to be someone who is capable of giving constructive, even painful, feedback. As Marcus Stafford, chief executive officer (CEO) at the Multiple Sclerosis Society of Western Australia, explains, "You might not like the feedback. But it is the only way you can develop yourself as a leader." Deliberate practice also requires intense concentration and focus. Even when the type of activity requires intense physical effort—as in athletic sports—the limiting factor is often more mental than physical. People are more likely to tire from mental strain than physical strain. That's why deliberate practice sessions are often only about two to three hours in duration.

Furthermore, and let's be realistic, deliberate practice isn't much fun. Although you should love what you do, amusement is not the intention of deliberate practice. What keeps the top performers going during the often-grueling practice sessions is not the enjoyment that they are having but the knowledge that they are improving and getting closer to their dream of superior performance.

Finally, there's just no getting around the fact that practice takes time; and often time is such a precious commodity that you don't feel you have enough of it to go around, let alone add more activities to your agenda. You may be familiar with the popularized notion that it takes "10,000 hours of practice" if you want to become an expert,[5] but the truth is there is no specific number. You have to put the time in, but don't make a big deal about the number of hours required. Perhaps the best rule of thumb comes from author and educator George Leonard, who wrote in his book *Mastery,* "We all aspire to mastery, but the path is always long and sometimes rocky, and it promises no quick and easy payoffs."[6] More important, mastery is about how you use your time to maximize your potential and learn your craft. That's why you have to learn to turn your workplace into a practice field, developing practice routines you can engage in during the regular hours you're at work.

PRACTICE WHILE YOU WORK

Let's say you get feedback that you're not listening attentively to others and that you'd be much more effective if you paid more attention to what people are saying. How, then, can you deliberately practice listening without adding more hours onto your already full and busy workday? What can you do intentionally to improve your listening skills using a designed learning activity while at work?

You begin by setting a purposeful stretch goal. The goal of any practice is to improve performance. It's about learning something new or fine-tuning an existing skill. It also should push you to the next level, not just be something that repeats what you do well. For example, you might set a goal of always clarifying your understanding of what others are saying before you respond to them. Next, you'll want to design or select a method for improvement. You need a process for improving—steps you will repeat to make sure that you do something correctly.

For instance, you decide to develop your listening skills by using the technique of active listening during your weekly staff meetings.[7] Following the meeting, you'll need to get feedback on how well you executed on the method and how close you got to your goal. That feedback can come from the other attendees in the meeting. You can, for example, ask everyone attending, "How did I do in actively listening? Did I hear you correctly?" If that's not realistic in your organization, you can also get it from a coach or a trusted colleague you've asked to observe you. This individual can give you feedback and tips on active listening. You could even video record the meeting and watch it afterward, which is what a lot of teachers, public speakers, and athletes do so that they can get a real-time sense of what happened. Video recording and playback may not always be practical, but when you can, the feedback you'll get from this method will be invaluable.

To benefit from practicing, you have to pay close attention to what you are doing. You should not be on autopilot during practice. You need to concentrate. Stay focused; use the technique you are experimenting with substantively. Although it might feel a little awkward, the point is to stick with the routine until it becomes second nature.

Using meetings for skill development is just one example of how you can take one of your regular activities and turn it into a practice area for leadership. There are many other ways to bring deliberate practice into the workplace. Analyzing case studies and role-playing, for instance, are both terrific ways to safely practice how to respond to critical incidents.

Nick Martin and Georgia DiMatteo were both involved in an ongoing leadership development program at the University of Delaware. Nick was quite comfortable with the leadership practice of Challenge the Process that Georgia found problematic, whereas Georgia was very comfortable when it came to Encourage the Heart but Nick shied away from doing it. So they decided to help each other practice deliberately by becoming accountability partners. Both set stretch goals for becoming better leaders, and then they consulted with each other about strategies for using their respective weak leadership practice in settings where they both were. Following those interactions they met, often simply over a cup of coffee, offering feedback about their intentions, how well they felt they used the leadership behaviors, what they might have done better, and what they were going to work on next. Georgia says, "We also like to tweak the learning as we go; we try to push each other even if it's just a little bit further." While constructively critical, they were supportive of each of their efforts and the progress made in becoming better leaders.

YOU CAN'T IGNORE YOUR WEAKNESSES

These days you hear a lot about how you should ignore your weaknesses and how you should find someone else who's good at what you're not and partner with that person to accommodate your weakness. Although it may be decent operational advice, that message is not consistent with what researchers on expertise have found. They have shown, across a variety of occupations and professions, that only by working at what you can't do can you expect to become the expert you aspire to be.[8]

If you want to be the best leader you can be, you will have to attend to your weaknesses. You can't delegate or assign to others those leadership behaviors you aren't comfortable doing. If you do, you'll get to be only as good as your weakest skill. Although you may never get as good as someone else at everything you do, by continuously practicing, practicing, and practicing, you can improve. You will also gain an appreciation for why persistence is another one of those attributes that differentiate the best from the wannabes. The very best in life never tire of doing what they can to get even better.

Consider what Phil Jackson, head coach for 11 National Basketball Association (NBA) Championship teams, said about legendary basketball superstar Michael Jordan:

> The weakest part of Michael's game on the offensive end was his shooting, so he obviously mastered something that everyone said he couldn't do when he came out of college. He did it by shooting, and shooting, and shooting, and shooting, consistently. The other thing that

people told him was that he wasn't really a good defensive player and he found a way to not only become a good defensive player but the best defensive player in the NBA. This guy said, "Those are my weaknesses and I'm going to figure out how to make those my strengths," and he did.[9]

It seems obvious that you can't ignore your weaknesses. Brian Brim, a senior practice consultant with the Gallup Organization, explains that ignoring weaknesses doesn't banish them, and doing so often just makes them worse because they'll continue to stand in the way of what you want to accomplish. "We have to deal with them so they'll quit dogging us," Brian says.[10]

When you begin learning to be a better leader, you don't need to start with the most difficult, scariest, or most challenging behavior or skill. Get started by making progress on something you think you can improve if you put your mind to it and are willing to practice deliberately. Don't keep overlooking the things you know you should be improving but just seem too hard, so you put them on the back burner. Seeing improvement in some areas may be just what you need to build up your confidence to tackle the competencies that need the most development.

THE KEY MESSAGE AND ACTION

The key message of this chapter is this: You can't get any better at leading, or at anything else for that matter, without practice. Moreover, the time spent practicing won't amount to much unless you adhere to some deliberate steps. Knowing your strengths and building upon them is important, but so is realizing that you are weak in some areas and that you must address them. The mantra for the twenty-first-century learner is this: "No matter how good I am, I can always get better."

SELF-COACHING ACTION

Make a list in your leadership journal of one or more leadership skills you would like to improve. It could be something you do pretty well, or it could be something that needs improvement. Now break that skill down into some of its essential chunks.[11] For example, let's say it's presentation skills, and some of the components involve eye contact, gestures, the tone of voice, stories, visuals, and the like. Pick one or two of these chunks you'd like to get better at, and decide on one method you'd like to practice. In the presentation skills example, it might be making eye contact. Make this your initial improvement target, and find a practice field where you can work on it (e.g., a weekly staff meeting). Be clear about why getting better is important to you and your team, organization, colleagues, or customers so that you can stay motivated in making this improvement.

Also identify someone who is willing to help you and ask that person to observe you when you practice. Set an improvement goal that represents a small win and allows for learning and recalibrating based on the feedback you'll receive. Don't worry about getting it right the first time. Just stay focused on your overall improvement objective and be willing to persist. Put in the time necessary to make this new behavior a natural part of your repertoire. In the presentation skills example, that might be practicing eye contact at each of your next three meetings. After each trial, figure out what worked and didn't work in this process so that you can apply those lessons to your next improvement target. Make notes about your practice experiences in your leadership journal.

Once you feel comfortable with your first skills chunk, move on to the next one.

CHAPTER 18

CONTEXT MATTERS

L enny Lind, among his other professional endeavors, is a coffee farmer in El Salvador. We were working together with Lenny on a conference, and we started exploring the lessons Lenny was learning from farming and how they applied to developing leaders. Lenny related how his agronomist, Luis Gutiérrez, was insistent that each plant would flourish with a *buena casa*—a good house—in which to grow. That meant that the holes into which they planted coffee seedlings had to be dug deep and filled with quality soil and nutrients. Although it would be cheaper to dig a shallow hole and use lower-quality materials, the plants could thrive and produce exceptional crops over the long term only if they took root from the beginning in a *buena casa*.

The same goes for human beings. When the environment in which people live and work provides the essential conditions and support for growth and development, people thrive. When the conditions are poor, and the support is lacking, people struggle and seldom reach their full potential. When there's a rich culture of leadership in an organization, leaders emerge, grow, and succeed. They prosper and contribute because they get the care and attention they need to become exemplary.

Ellen Langer, psychology professor at Harvard University, is one of the world's leading experts on how context influences people's decisions, actions, and well-being.[1] She offers this observation: "If you want to gain control over your life, the first step is to ask who controls the context. Then find ways to generate the kind of context that will help you do the things you want to do. By being aware of the context, and making more mindful choices about it, you can become the master of your fate."[2]

In one classic experiment, Ellen and fellow researchers gave plants to nursing home residents. In the experimental group, the residents were encouraged to make their own decisions about the care of the plants, while in the comparison group the residents were told that the nurses would take care of the plants. Those in the experimental group were also encouraged to make other decisions, such as where to receive visitors and on what night they wanted to see a movie; again, those in the comparison group were not encouraged one way or the other to make any decisions about such matters.

What happened was dramatic. Eighteen months after the experiments were over, those in the experimental condition had significantly improved their health and lowered their mortality rate. The health of those in the comparison group, however, had worsened. As a result of being mindful of the decisions they made by themselves, those who took more responsibility for their lives in the nursing home showed "more initiative and were significantly more active, vigorous, and sociable" than those in the comparison group.[3] Researchers randomly assigned people to the different groups, so it wasn't the characteristics of the residents that made the difference; it was the context that the organization created.

It's important to be mindful of the context in which you live and work if you want to grow and develop your leadership competencies. It would be ideal if you could be in an organizational setting that cultivated leadership and provided lots of practice opportunities. But, sometimes you are planted in less-than-ideal, even harsh, conditions, and in those contexts you'll have to develop and foster your own culture of leadership.

CULTIVATE A CULTURE OF LEADERSHIP

Context matters. You know intimately from your daily experience how much context influences your thoughts and behavior. For example, when you're at a theme park, such as Disney World, Efteling, Lotte World, or LEGOLAND, you know that you're there to laugh, scream with delight, and play. But when you're in a house of worship, library, or funeral home, those same behaviors are probably frowned upon, to say the least. Name a context, and you will find out quickly how you are supposed to behave.

When applied to the workplace, context is often talked about as the organizational culture. It's a somewhat elusive concept, but according to Edgar Schein, emeritus professor at Massachusetts Institute of Technology's (MIT) Sloan School of Management and one of the leading authorities on the topic, organizational culture can be best understood as having three levels. First are artifacts and these are the things you can see: structures, processes, and observed behavior. You see them in dress, interior design, furniture, formal management systems, organization charts, employee perks, company publications, and the like. The second level is espoused beliefs and values. These are the ideals, aspirations, visions, and ideologies the organization and its leaders champion. You hear and see these beliefs in speeches, employee orientations, training programs, and posters on the wall. The third level of organizational culture is "underlying, taken-for-granted beliefs and values" that are not expressed overtly in speech or text. They're implicit rather than explicit, but they are often the most influential factors in how people think, feel, and act.[4]

To illustrate, in Chapter 5 we talked about fixed and growth mindsets and how each influences learning and performance. Imagine that a fixed mindset was the norm in an organization; the pervasive assumption was that employees were fixed in their abilities and fundamentally could not change their basic behaviors. Alternatively, imagine that the dominant norm was a growth mindset. Wouldn't these two different mindsets undoubtedly influence the decisions and choices made about the ways in which people were recruited, managed, and developed?

This is exactly what researchers find when they examine the differences between organizations with growth-mindset cultures versus fixed-mindset cultures. In growth-mindset organizations there is a "culture of development." Leaders believe in people's ability to grow and to learn from their mistakes. They see their employees as more committed to learning and they see their organizations as having more leadership potential than in fixed-mindset workplaces.[5] If you want to become the best leader you can be, you will benefit immensely from working in an organization with a culture of leadership—a culture in which the artifacts, espoused beliefs and values, and underlying assumptions are supportive of leadership development.

CHARACTERISTICS OF A CULTURE OF LEADERSHIP

What are the attributes of a culture in which leaders are most likely to thrive and be productive? We recently posed this question to more than 200 leadership educators and developers.[6]

Four major clusters of cultural attributes emerged from their responses: trust, opportunities for learning, support for risk and failure, and models of exemplary leadership.

The most frequently occurring word that characterized a culture of leadership was *trust*. If leaders are going to grow and thrive, people need to trust one another. They need to feel safe around one other, able to be open and honest with one another. They need to support people's growth, have one another's backs, and be there to lift others up when they fall or stumble. They need to be able to collaborate and cheer on everyone. They need to show respect for differences and be open to alternative viewpoints and backgrounds. A culture of leadership that supports collaborative behavior is going to be more hospitable to the development of leaders than one that is internally competitive and focuses on a winner-take-all approach to selecting and promoting leaders.

Organizations with a culture of leadership are fanatical about making learning a priority and providing a variety of systematic opportunities for learning. The global consulting firm Aon Hewitt found that 100 percent of the top companies for leaders had a "strong reputation for internally cultivating talent throughout the organization" compared to only 66 percent of other companies.[7] In its research on the factors that are of the most interest to high-quality job candidates, Gallup found that the best people are "attracted to roles that provide opportunities to learn and grow. Their ideal job would feature professional development or growth opportunities."[8] Organizations with strong cultures of leadership offer many formal and informal opportunities for developing their people, such as classroom-based learning programs, online learning options, external seminars, as well as mentoring and coaching. Rotational job assignments or special projects also challenge people to develop themselves. Designed feedback is encouraged, and learning is recognized and rewarded, making it something in which people want to participate.

Learning also requires taking risks—doing things you've never done before, challenging yourself to take on new assignments, addressing your weaknesses, and stretching into areas of discomfort. In cultures that develop exemplary leaders, there's not only tolerance for risk but also support and encouragement to experiment. When you try out new behaviors, you don't get it right the first time. You mess up a lot. If you are going to venture into the unknown, you have to be a bit courageous, and you have to know that there's support there to take that step. It's a lot easier to risk when you know there's someone to catch you if you fall.

Organizations that encourage innovation also provide time for working on projects outside of formal responsibilities, which can only enhance people's capabilities. Such environments nurture curiosity, which is a necessary antecedent to thinking outside the box. Recent studies at the Center for Neuroscience at the University of California, Davis, reveal that being curious prepares the brain for learning, including information that people might ordinarily consider boring or difficult. Curiosity also makes learning a more gratifying experience by stimulating the brain circuits associated with reward and pleasure.[9]

Finally, models of exemplary leadership are needed. You have to be able to see exemplary leadership in action to learn to produce it yourself. You need to see people in the organization model exemplary leadership and support leadership development at all levels. You need to hear stories about how leaders who lived the espoused values were successful and rewarded. You need access to those with experience and expertise. You need to see people held accountable for actions that are inconsistent with espoused beliefs. You also need to see and hear examples of leaders at all levels. From frontline supervisor to senior executive, from customer to individual contributor, everyone is viewed as capable of leading and encouraged to lead.

Although other factors can contribute to a culture of leadership, these four are the most salient. If you have the good fortune to be part of an organization that embodies them, you are off to a great start. If you don't, do not despair. There are a few ways you can tend to the soil yourself to enable the plant (that is, you) to grow heartily.

BUILD YOUR OWN *BUENA CASA*

When asked what advice she'd give new college grads, Jan Singer, chief executive officer (CEO) of apparel maker Spanx, replied, "Never stop learning. If you have it all figured out, you're dead. You have to be open, and you have to listen and learn. You may feel a bit exhausted from all the learning in college, but find what energizes you and keep learning."[10]

You may not have the good fortune of working in an organization deeply committed to cultivating a culture of leadership or in places where formal leadership training and development opportunities are even available. No matter. That doesn't change the fact that the best leaders are good at continuously sharpening their skills. In many places, you will have to build your own *buena casa*—to cultivate a culture of leadership wherever you are.

How do you do that? Use the culture of leadership attributes as guidelines for building your own context. For instance, who are the people around you whom you trust, and what can they do to support your leadership development journey? With whom can you be open and honest about your strengths and areas for improvement as a leader? Whom do you know who has some expertise you could learn from, and how can you tap into his or her experience and ultimately his or her network? Where are opportunities for you to get some feedback on your current level of skills as a leader?[11]

How can you support yourself for taking a risk, possibly making a mistake, and moving outside of your comfort zone? Consider taking small steps rather than huge leaps—or even one step at a time when it comes to really stretching yourself. If you know some folks who you think are quite comfortable innovating and taking risks, get together with them, and talk about both how they do this and what you might be able to do (or get away with). The more serious you are about learning, the more questions you should ask.

In addition to reflecting on your own personal-best leadership experience, think about all the best leaders you have known. Seek them out and ask them to share their learning journeys. How did they learn to lead or develop particular leadership skills? What advice would they have for you? Even better, find out whether they would be willing to help you develop that same competency.

The bottom line is that if you want a plant to flourish, you have to build a *buena casa* in which the seedling can take root and thrive for the long term. You have to do the same for yourself to succeed as a leader.

THE KEY MESSAGE AND ACTION

The key message of this chapter is this: Context affects your ability to grow and thrive as a leader—big time. Environments where you find trust and respect are critical, as are opportunities for learning, support for risk and failure, and role models from whom you can learn more about exemplary leadership. Sometimes you'll have to take charge of developing your own culture of leadership.

SELF-COACHING ACTION

Find another person who, like you, is interested in learning. Although you want to focus on leadership, and he or she might wish to do the same or something else, that doesn't matter so long as you both have a commitment to learning. Become accountability partners (or learning buddies). Select one of the development actions you've already identified in your leadership journal, and tell your partner what you want to learn and why it is important. Identify specific actions you are going to take in the next 30 and 90 days. Then, put a date on the calendar when you'll connect with each other in person (preferably), by phone, or virtually. The sole job of your accountability partner is simply to ask, "Did you do what you said you would do?" and then you both can take it from there.

CHAPTER 19

LEARNING LEADERSHIP MUST BE A DAILY HABIT

We had the good fortune to do a couple of workshops with Jim Whittaker, the first American to summit Mt. Everest, the earth's highest mountain. Jim also led the first team of Americans to summit K2, the second-highest mountain in the world. And he didn't just climb mountains. Among his many other outdoor adventures, twice Jim captained his sailboat in the 2,400-mile Victoria to Maui International Yacht Race and made the 20,000-mile voyage from Washington to Australia four times. Jim is also an experienced executive, spending 25 years with Recreational Equipment Inc. (REI), initially as its first full-time employee and eventually retiring as its president and chief executive officer (CEO).

After all the adventures he's had, when Jim reflects on his philosophy of life, he offers this observation: "It has nothing to do with thrill-seeking. It's about making the most of every moment, about stretching your own boundaries, about being willing to learn constantly, and putting yourself in situations where learning is possible—sometimes even critical to your survival. Being out on the edge, with everything at risk, is where you learn—and grow—the most."[1]

Jim has nailed it. The best leaders aren't doing what they're doing for the power or the fame or the thrill. They're doing what they're doing to learn and grow and make the most of what they can offer to other people, their communities, and their organizations. "Being willing to learn constantly" is exactly what this book discusses. It's about making the most of every opportunity you have to learn to lead. It's about stretching yourself and being willing to learn continually from the challenges in front of you. It's about stepping out to the edge of your capabilities and asking a little bit more of yourself.

The first step up that mountain to becoming the best leader you can be is taking charge of your leadership development. As we said in Chapter 18, it would be ideal if every organization had a culture of leadership, and if every leader you ever worked with were exemplary. More than likely, though, you're going to have to be the person who drives your learning agenda.

MAKE LEARNING LEADERSHIP A DAILY HABIT

Harry Kraemer, former chairman and CEO of Baxter International and now a clinical professor at Northwestern University's Kellogg School of Management, has taught us a lot about what it means to take learning seriously. Every day, usually at the end of the day when work and family activities have concluded, Harry spends 15 to 30 minutes reflecting on "the day that is coming to a close, the impact I have made, and the impact that others have made on me."[2] He asks himself some questions about what he said he'd do, what he actually did, what went well, what didn't, what he'd do differently, what he learned that had an impact on how he lives going forward, and so on. Reflecting on his day is not something Harry started doing recently. He's been doing it for 35 years, 24/7, 365. That's more than 12,500 times. It's a habit with Harry—an excellent habit.

Very early on in his career, Harry made becoming a better leader a daily habit. "No one," he says, "is beyond becoming their best self. At this point in my life, I have been CFO [chief financial officer], president, CEO and chairman of a $12 billion global health-care company, with a combined tenure of 11 years at the top of Baxter International. Currently, I'm an executive partner with Madison Dearborn Partners, a Chicago-based private-equity firm, and despite the success I've been lucky to have, I remain just as committed to being my best self as I did when I was starting out in one of those cubicles as a junior analyst, decades ago."[3]

The most meaningful and important way you can take charge of your learning and become your best self is to make learning to be a better leader a daily habit, just as Harry does. Your daily learning habits don't have to be the same as his, but you need to have processes that are just as regular.

Lewis Howes knows a thing or two about habits. He's a former pro football player and two-sport all-American, as well as a member of the U.S. men's national handball team. He's also the host of *The School of Greatness* and was a top 100 entrepreneur under 30. Lewis makes the following point about the relationship between becoming exemplary and developing habits: "Greatness is not the exclusive domain of the talented. Greatness is the result of visionaries who persevere, focus, believe, and *prepare*. It is a habit, not a birthright."[4] Repeat: Greatness is a habit, not a birthright. Lewis goes on to say, "Here's the thing about positive habits: it isn't that important which habits you practice, as long as they are beneficial and they work for you. What matters is that you commit to them and that you do them every day. Just like developing hustle is really about doing the work, practicing positive habits is about committing to a routine."[5] Among the habits on Lewis's daily list are "Wake up early and say thank you for being alive another day" and "Make my bed!" Also on his daily list are "Work with a coach and mentors" and "Constantly learn new information and skills."[6] These may not seem like the stuff of greatness, but they are for Lewis. His point is that to become the best at anything, you have to engage in routine actions that move you toward your goals. None of these things by themselves is difficult. What is challenging is doing them every day.

Learning leadership is not something you add on to your already-busy schedule when you get around to it. It's not something you do on a weekend or once a month at a retreat. It's not something that gets cut from the calendar when times are tough. It's something you do as automatically and instinctively as your other important priorities in the day. It's something that happens as routinely as checking your e-mail, texting a colleague, or conducting a meeting. It's something you consider essential to your personal success. And just like physical exercise, you have to do it daily to get fit and stay in shape.

HABITS SHAPE YOUR LIFE

New York Times reporter Charles Duhigg in *The Power of Habit* explains that habit formation happens in a three-step loop. "First, there is a *cue*, a trigger that tells your brain to go into automatic mode and which habit to use. Then there is a *routine*, which can be physical or mental or emotional. Finally, there is a *reward*, which helps your brain figure out if this particular reward is worth remembering for the future. Over time, this loop—cue, routine, reward; cue, routine, reward—becomes more and more automatic."[7] The Golden Rule of Habit Change, according to Charles, is "You can't extinguish a bad habit, you can only change it."[8] How do you change it? You use the same cue and reward, but you change the routine. You can also employ the same three-step loop to build new habits where none currently exists.

For Harry Kraemer, the cue is the quiet time at the end of the day. The routine is 15 to 30 minutes of reflecting with a standard set of questions. The reward is learning. Repeating that process day after day after day cements it as a habit.

It's important that you understand how this process works for you, because, as Gretchen Rubin points out in her book *Better Than Before*, "Habits are the invisible architecture of our daily life. We repeat 40 percent of our behavior almost daily, so our habits shape our existence, and our future. If we change our habits, we change our lives."[9] It's a bold statement, and it happens to be true. If someone can replace an old habit, such as eating sweets when stressed, with a new habit, such as taking a walk, that simple act will improve long-term health. If someone can replace an old habit of interrupting others when they are talking with a new one of active listening, that new habit will improve long-term leadership effectiveness. If someone can replace negative self-talk when confronting a challenge with a positive affirmation, that new habit will improve learning to lead.

But the *if* in those sentences is a big *IF*. Adopting new habits and changing old ones are not easy. Less than half of New Year's resolutions make it past six months. And everyone who studies habit formation will tell you that there isn't one style that fits all. You have to identify for yourself the cues, routines, and rewards that work for you. The most important point is this: Learning leadership must be an integral part of your daily life. It must become a habit.

Researchers have found that what makes people feel motivated at work is that they make daily progress, even a little progress, on meaningful work.[10] People feel most energized, engaged, joyful, and creative on those days when they see forward movement on something that's meaningful to them. Forming good habits that enable you to assess the progress you make every day will serve to motivate you to do even more meaningful work.

BUILD GOOD HABITS WITH ACTIVE QUESTIONS

Executive coach and author Marshall Goldsmith, who has worked with more than 80 CEOs from some of the world's top companies, writes with Mark Reiter in their book *Triggers* that asking *active questions* each day is a "magic move." It's a very simple, yet powerful, way to review how you've done each day on keeping your commitments to do something to be a better leader. "The act of self-questioning—so simple, so misunderstood, so infrequently pursued—changes everything."[11] It's a daily habit that makes a big difference in sticking to your plans to become your best leadership self.

In active questioning, Marshall recommends that you start the question with "Did I do my best to . . ." followed by whatever action you intend to take. This form of questioning primes you to think about a high standard of performance. It's an active question about something you did, as compared with passive questions—questions that ask about a static condition. For example, "Do you have clear goals?" is a passive question. It asks about what is or isn't a current state. An active version would be "Did you do your best to set clear goals for yourself?"[12]

To test the impact of active questions, Marshall and Northwestern University marketing professor Kelly Goldsmith set up a controlled study with employees going through a training program on engaging themselves at work and home. The training consisted of a two-hour session held every day for 10 consecutive days. The researchers asked one group of participants at the end of each day four *passive* questions—such as "How happy were you today?" They asked the other group four questions every day for 10 consecutive days after the training, but the questions were *active* questions, such as "Did you do your best to be happy?" At the beginning of the two-week period, and again at the end, the researchers asked a control group, which received no training, four questions about their levels of "happiness, meaning, building positive relationships, and engagement."[13]

After the 10 days, as you might expect, the control group showed little change from their baseline two weeks prior. Although both the passive-questions and the active-questions groups showed positive improvement, the active questions produced *twice* the effectiveness compared with the passive questions. These results demonstrated that some follow-up is better than none, but active questioning has a greater impact than passive questioning.

Leaders spend a lot of time trying to change organizations and other people. Although change is the work of leaders, when implementing change leaders can lose sight of the fact that the only person's behavior anyone can control is his or her own. Changing your behavior and building new skills aren't easy. They're very hard work. That's why it's critical to make learning leadership a habit. Good habits pave the pathway to exemplary leadership. Whatever routine you choose for yourself—whether it's daily reflections, daily self-questioning, or something else— the act of engaging daily in learning leadership is essential to becoming the best leader you can be.

THE KEY MESSAGE AND ACTION

The key message of this chapter is this: The best leaders know that they have to learn constantly—that learning leadership is a lifelong endeavor. No matter how many summits they've ascended, they know that you have to take a step every day to improve—one reflection at a time, one question at a time, and one lesson at a time. When all is said and done, you are the person in charge of your development. You have to commit to the habit of learning something new every day and the habit of assessing your progress every day.

SELF-COACHING ACTION

Start asking yourself each day some active questions. Building on Marshall's routine, here are five questions that you could use to check in on how you are doing in applying the fundamentals of learning to lead:

1. Did I do my best to remain positive about my abilities today?
2. Did I do my best to focus on exciting future possibilities today?
3. Did I do my best to challenge and stretch myself today?
4. Did I do my best to learn from other people today?
5. Did I do my best to practice a new leadership skill today?

Regardless of whether your answer to these questions is yes or no, consider the reason you answered the way you did. If you say yes, record in your leadership journal what you did so that you can continue to do those things that affirm that you did your best. If you say no, think about what you could start doing that would cause you to say yes the next day.

Try formulating your own "Did I do my best to" active questions. Apply this technique to your particular learning needs. At the end of the day, using a 1 (low) to 10 (high) scale, rate yourself in your leadership journal on how you did on each question. Track your progress. What's important about daily questioning is not so much the specific numbers but the fact that you make this process a daily habit.

If possible, find someone you know and trust to be your partner in doing this. Tell this person that you're working on building a new habit and that you need his or her help. Ask that individual to call you every day for just three to five minutes and to ask you, "Did you do your best to . . . ?" Rate yourself on a scale of 1 to 10, and tell that person what you gave yourself and why. Perhaps someone at work could be your partner and you could check in with each other for five minutes every morning. If calling or talking with someone every day doesn't work, then use your smartphone as your assistant. Put a daily reminder in your phone, and have it send you an alert at the same time every day. When you get that alert, stop and answer the question that you selected. The point is that you have to do it daily to see the change. That's why they call it a habit.

PART VII

COMMIT TO BECOMING THE BEST

The proof that you know leadership is in the doing of it. It's not just in making the decisions to act; it's about acting on the decisions you make.

The best way to take those actions is to do little things every day that make meaningful progress on your work as a leader. Small acts accumulate and provide momentum. You have to freely choose the actions you take, go public with your choices, and then make sure it's hard to reverse course. When you take these steps, you build your commitment to becoming the best leader you can be.

Becoming exemplary in any endeavor is hard work. Leadership is no exception. Making extraordinary things happen requires extraordinary effort. There's a tremendous payoff if you are willing to pay the price. Be prepared to make sacrifices and even to suffer at times if you aspire to be exemplary.

To become the best leader, you must be positive and hopeful about your future. High levels of personal energy and enthusiasm are necessary. There's a *way*, but you can sustain your leadership development journey only when you also have the *will*.

In the closing chapter we urge you to:

* Do what you decide to do.
* Work hard and move forward in small steps.
* Sustain commitment.
* Keep hope alive.

CHAPTER 20

IT'S NOT HOW YOU START; IT'S HOW YOU FINISH

The five fundamentals discussed in this book provide a framework for creating the context in which you can become the best leader you can be—a mindset that promotes continuous growth and development.

To become the best you have to *believe you can.* You have the power and capacity to be exemplary, and you need to believe that deep down. Do not let anyone tell you anything different. You have to *aspire to excel.* You need a set of values and a vision that are greater than you are, and you need to think long term. You have to *challenge yourself* to go beyond your current level of performance and experiment with new and different ways of doing things. Your growth opportunities start at the edges of your current capacity. You have to *engage support* to learn and grow. Learning leadership is not something you do all by yourself. You need other people to help you become your best. Finally, you have to *practice deliberately.* Bringing out the best in yourself takes practice, and practice takes time. You have to make learning a daily habit.

Making learning a daily habit is where you start. However, there's more, because it's not just how you start; it's also how you finish. Like anything in life, the evidence that you are leading, and leading well, will come based on the actions you take not just on the first day but also through to the last day.

LEADING IS DOING

Twelve frogs were sitting on a log. Seven frogs decided to jump into the pond. How many frogs remain on the log?

What's your answer? Is it seven, five, twelve, none? The correct answer is twelve. Why? Because the seven frogs only *decided* to jump; they didn't actually take the leap. There's an enormous difference between deciding and doing. It's like the old saying goes: "To know and not to do is not yet to know." That's why so few New Year's resolutions are kept very long. You can decide to live a healthier life, to lose weight, to exercise more each day, and to keep track of your calorie consumption, but that's not the same thing as doing each of these things day after day after day.

The same is true for leadership. Learning about leadership and leaders is not the same as leading. Deciding to be an exemplary leader is not the same as being one. Leading is doing, and you have to *do* leadership to be a leader. In fact, one of the consistent findings in our research is that for others to consider you credible, you have to *do what you say you will do.*[1] You have to follow through on promises, keep commitments, and put your money where your mouth is. Your actions speak louder than your words.

You need to make leading a daily habit. You need to do something every day to learn more about leading, and you need to put those lessons into practice every day. You need to jump into the pond, demonstrate that you know how to stay afloat, and over time become a more capable swimmer.

Sergey Nikiforov, now vice president and chief evangelist at enterprise software solutions company GOAPPO, pondered this challenge, explaining to us that the question of "Where do I start becoming a better leader?" had been "nagging me for some time." Sergey assumed that he had to do something grand and ambitious to demonstrate he was a leader, but then something else dawned on him.

> I found that every day I had an opportunity to make a small difference. I could have coached someone better, I could have listened better, I could have been more positive toward people, I could have said "thank you" more often, I could have . . . the list just went on.
>
> At first, I was a bit overwhelmed with the discovery of how many opportunities I had in a single day to act as a better leader. But as I have gotten to put these ideas into practice I have been pleasantly surprised by how much improvement I have been able to make by being more conscientious and intentional about acting as a leader.

Sergey discovered that it wasn't the every-once-in-a-while, transformational acts that demonstrated his leadership. It was the little things that he did day in and day out. Without knowing it, his actions were exactly those things that enable people to experience a good day at work. That's how we recommend you continue along your leadership journey—finding opportunities every day to make a small difference.

HOW TO HAVE A GOOD DAY

Everyone wants to have a good day at work. Researchers and authors Teresa Amabile and Steven Kramer discovered a significant way to make this happen. "If a person is motivated and happy at the end of the workday, it's a good bet that he or she made some progress. If the person drags out of the office disengaged and joyless, a setback is most likely to blame."[2] For example, they found that on good days progress was made 76 percent of the time, but on bad days, progress was made only

25 percent of the time. On bad days, 67 percent of the time there were setbacks, but on good days, there were setbacks only 13 percent of the time. The secret to having a good day, then, is to make progress on your work each day and to prevent setbacks. But there's a catch. The work has to matter to you so that the progress feels meaningful. Making headway on stuff that you don't care about doesn't increase your motivation, engagement, or sense of fulfillment.

Making progress every day may not always be as easy as you'd like it to be. Stuff happens that can seriously disrupt your flow—a broken water heater, a computer crash, a discouraging comment, an uncooperative colleague, or an unappreciative boss, to mention a few—but the goal remains to find ways to make meaningful progress every day.

How do you do this? Most often, the little things enable a sense of progress. Big wins are great but they rarely happen, and the good news, according to Teresa and Steven is "that even small wins boost inner work life tremendously. Many of the progress events our research participants reported represented only minor steps forward. Yet they often evoked outsize positive reactions."[3] Success comes by taking regular small steps forward, and disappointment is more likely to occur when you attempt giant leaps.

Sergey discovered exactly that. He learned he could "make a small difference" every day. You have the opportunity to do many little things to demonstrate your leadership. You can tell a story that illustrates an important value that should guide decisions and actions. You can spend a few minutes helping people understand the important part their work plays in the bigger picture. You can provide constructive feedback on someone's performance. You can coach someone who is struggling with a new assignment. You can publicly recognize someone for an action that set the example for others on the team.

One of the reasons why we've provided the self-coaching actions in this book is to break learning leadership down into some manageable chunks. It's an application of the small wins or progress principle, and by engaging in these, you will be making incremental progress toward becoming an exemplary leader. By themselves, these actions may seem small, but the cumulative effect will be hugely positive.

SUSTAINING COMMITMENT

When you make headway on something that's important to you, it encourages you to take other actions that help you make meaningful progress. It makes it easier and easier to take the next step on the journey. To act is to commit oneself. There's no sitting on the log. It's about jumping in the pond. With each action, you further commit yourself—and you start getting more comfortable and confident in the water. To sustain commitment, you need to do three things.

1. *Make Free and Informed Choices:* If you and another person are sitting at a table, predicting the probability of pulling a number out of a hat, you will predict that you have a much better chance of winning if you know that it's *your* hand that will do the picking rather than the other person's—even though the odds are statistically the same. People believe if they do the choosing, their chances of winning are greater than if someone else does the choosing.[4] That's why making a free and informed choice is the first step in the commitment-making process.

    Leadership is a choice. Either you choose to be one, or you don't. You have other options in life. But when you make that choice, you are taking responsibility for that action. Essentially, you are saying something like this: "It was *my* choice. No one forced me. I had alternatives. I had a realistic picture of what one option would entail over another, and I chose this one. In the end, there is no one or no factor other than myself to 'blame' for this decision or action."

What's important in the choice process, however, is making sure that you closely examine the alternatives. Feeling forced into leadership roles fails the test of choice—so don't expect it to build commitment. Consider your alternatives. Consider the pros and cons. Get a realistic picture of what's involved before signing up.

Therefore, the first question is, "Am I making a free choice to become an exemplary leader?"

2. *Make Your Choices Visible to Others:* Once you've made the choice to lead, commit yourself further by telling someone else about what you decided to do. Commitment is more likely when you make your choices visible. By announcing your choices to others and by making the subsequent actions visible, you offer tangible, undeniable evidence of your commitment to the cause. You also become subject to other people's review and observation. Testimonials in behavior change programs, such as Alcoholics Anonymous or Weight Watchers, make an individual's level of commitment quite visible to others. Stating one's days or years of sobriety or stepping on the scale with others watching is more binding than the promise to do better next week.

Visibility makes it nearly impossible for people to deny their choices or to claim that they forgot about them. We've recommended more than once that you work with a colleague, partner, or coach. When you work with someone else, you're more likely to follow through than if you were to attempt something all by yourself. The value of a personal trainer at your local fitness club, for example, is not just that trainers have exercises that they get you to do. That's certainly useful. But equally important—if not more important—is that when you hire a personal trainer, you're just more likely to go to the gym and work out.

Acting as a leader is clearly a public act. Keeping it to yourself is impossible. Take the next step and publicly declare that you're going to do all you can to be the best leader you can be.

The second question is, "How am I going to make my decision to become an exemplary leader visible?"

3. *Make Your Choices Hard to Revoke:* For you to become committed to a choice, making the decision visible is necessary but insufficient. The choice must also be difficult to change or take back. Choices that are hard to change increase your investment in the decision and the follow-through. Choices that are easy to reverse are taken lightly; ones that are difficult to undo are treated very seriously.

Think about this example for a moment. Let's suppose that you have considered for a long time a move to the country. You keep telling your friends and family that you are sick of the smog, the traffic, and the congestion and that you are going to move. Periodically you've rented a vacation place out in the country for a week or two, but you never make the move. Then one day you decide to do it. Which of these options is harder to back out of: (a) renting the house in the country or (b) buying it? Leaders find ways to own, not just rent, decisions. Figuratively speaking, put your city house up for sale, and purchase that home in the country. Find ways to make the choice work going forward; make it difficult to retreat and go back to the beginning.

The third question to ask yourself is "What am I going to do to make my decision to become an exemplary leader hard to back out of?"

KEEP HOPE ALIVE

Becoming an exemplary leader requires your behavioral commitment. It's not something you do now and then when you feel like it. The people around you expect you to be the best leader you can be *every day*. They expect, and so should you, that when you commit to lead you are also committing yourself to doing it well.

None of this is easy, by any means. Leadership is hard work. It's challenging work. There are times when you will suffer. There will be conflicts and struggles. There will be cynics and critics who don't like what you do. There will be resistance to the changes you want to make. There will be times when you want to give up. As rewarding as it is, leadership can be exhausting. That's just the reality of leading. And no amount of coaching matters if you don't want to put in more than minimum effort.

That's why you have to keep your hope alive. The research clearly shows that people expect their leaders to be inspiring, upbeat, and energetic. No one wants to follow a negative, downbeat, and lethargic person. You won't want to follow yourself if you're that way. Why would you? Despite all the negativity, cynicism, and struggles that might surround you, you have to sustain hope. Hope that you will overcome the challenges you face. Hope that you can continue to learn and grow. Hope that things will get better.

Hope is not just a matter of "Where there's a will, there's a way." This old folk wisdom is only half correct, said psychologist and researcher Charles (Rick) Snyder. Hope, he found, "is the sum of the mental willpower and waypower that you have for your goals."[5] This definition stresses hope's three essential ingredients. First you have to have a goal—something you want to attain or obtain. Then you have to have the willpower, the "reservoir of determination," and third, the waypower, the "mental plans or road maps that guide hopeful thought" to get you to your goals whatever the obstacles that you might face. This perspective leads to several questions that you need to ask yourself: Are you clear about what you want to attain or obtain as a leader? Do you have the energy to sustain yourself as you move toward your goals? Do you have a plan of action on how you are going to reach your goals? To have hope, you need to answer yes to all three of these questions.

People with high hope are not Pollyannas. They are not blind to the realities of the present. If something isn't working or if the current methods aren't effective, they don't ignore it, cross their fingers, or just redouble their efforts. They assess the situation and find new ways to reach the goals. And if the goals begin to recede rather than appear closer, people with hope re-sct their goals.[6] The other important thing to know about hope is that it is not something either you have or you don't. As Rick explained, "Hope is a learned way of thinking about oneself in relation to goals."[7] You can learn to be full of hope, just as you can learn to lead.

THE KEY MESSAGE

The key message of this chapter is this: Becoming the best leader you can be requires a mindset that promotes continuous growth—a mindset based on The Five Practices of Exemplary Leadership. You can't just decide to lead; you have to do leadership. You do that incrementally, in small steps that make meaningful progress every day. And you have to commit to leading by freely choosing your actions, going public with them, and making it difficult to back out of your actions. None of this is easy; it requires sustained effort and a hopeful outlook to continue the quest.

We are confident that you can become an even better leader than you are today. And when you use those skills to make extraordinary things happen, you will bring a lot more hope to those you lead. Your neighborhood, organization, and community and the world need this to be true.

NOTES

INTRODUCTION: THE WORLD NEEDS EXEMPLARY LEADERS

1. There are differing opinions on the exact years when the millennial generation begins and ends. We use the range from the Pew Research Center, which has done extensive research in this topic. See Richard Fry, "This Year, Millennials Will Overtake Baby Boomers," Pew Research Center, January 16, 2015, www .pewresearch.org/fact-tank/2015/01/16/this-year-millennials-will-overtake-baby-boomers.

2. Right Management, "Talent Management Challenges in an Era of Uncertainty," June 6, 2013, https://www.brighttalk.com/webcast/7991/72973/talent-management-challenges-in-era-of-uncertainty.

3. Shiza Shahid, "Outlook on the Global Agenda 2015: 3. Lack of Leadership," World Economic Forum, 2015, accessed January 5, 2016, http://reports.weforum.org/outlook-global-agenda-2015/top-10-trends-of-2015/3-lack-of-leadership/. This concern is equally distributed across the globe: 83 percent Asia, 85 percent Europe, 84 percent Latin America, 85 percent Middle East and North Africa, 92 percent North America, and 92 percent Sub-Saharan Africa.

4. Josh Bersin, Dimple Agarwal, Bill Pelster, and Jeff Schwartz, eds., *Global Human Capital Trends 2015: Leading in the New World of Work* (Westlake, TX: Deloitte University Press, 2015), 17, www2 .deloitte.com/content/dam/Deloitte/at/Documents/human-capital/ hc-trends-2015.pdf.

5. Executive Development Associates, *Trends in Executive Development 2014* (Oklahoma City, OK: Executive Development Associates and Pearson, 2014), 14, www.executivedevelopment.com/online-solutions/ product/trends-in-executive-development-2014.

6. Jack Zenger, "We Wait Too Long to Train Our Leaders," *Harvard Business Review*, December 17, 2012, https://hbr.org/2012/12/why- do-we-wait-so-long-to-trai%20wsletter_leadership&utm_medium= email&utm_campaign=leadership010813.

7. Edelman, "Trust around the World," 2015, accessed July 19, 2015, www.edelman.com/2015-edelman-trust-barometer/trust-around- world. Also see Edelman, 2015 *Edelman Trust Barometer Executive Summary* (Eldelman, 2015), www.edelman.com/insights/intellectual- property/2015-edelman-trust-barometer/trust-and-innovation-edelman- trust-barometer/executive-summary.

8. Unless otherwise noted, all quotations from individuals are from personal interviews or correspondence with the authors.

9. Universum, "Millennials: Understanding a Misunderstood Generation," 2015, http://universumglobal.com/millennials.

CHAPTER 1: LEADERS ARE BORN AND SO ARE YOU

1. For example, see Geoff Colvin, *Talent Is Overrated: What Really Separates World-Class Performers from Everybody Else* (New York: Penguin Group, 2010); and Daniel Coyle, *The Talent Code: Greatness Isn't Born. It's Grown. Here's How* (New York: Bantam Dell, 2009).

2. K. Anders Ericsson, ed., *The Road to Excellence: The Acquisition of Expert Performance in the Arts and Sciences, Sports, and Games* (Mahwah, NJ: Lawrence Erlbaum Associates, 1996); and K. Anders Ericsson, ed., *Development of Professional Expertise: Toward Mea- surement of Expert Performance and Design of Optimal Learning* (New York: Cambridge University Press, 2009).

3. Heidi Grant Halvorson, *Succeed: How We Can Reach Our Goals,* reprint ed. (New York: Penguin Group, 2011).

4. To learn more about our research involving personal-best experiences and on the practices of exemplary leadership we derived from these cases, see James M. Kouzes and Barry Z. Posner, *The Leadership Challenge: How to Make Extraordinary Things Happen in Organizations,* 5th ed. (San Francisco: The Leadership Challenge, A Wiley Brand, 2012).

5. *Merriam-Webster Unabridged online,* s.v. "lead," n.d., accessed June 7, 2015, http://unabridged.merriam-webster.com.

6. K. Anders Ericsson, "The Influence of Experience and Deliberate Practice on the Development of Superior Expert Performance," in *The Cambridge Handbook of Expertise and Expert Performance,* ed. K. Anders Ericsson, Neil Charness, Paul J. Feltovich, and Robert R. Hoffman (New York: Cambridge University Press, 2006), 699.

7. Nancy J. Adler, "Want to Be an Outstanding Leader? Keep a Journal," *Harvard Business Review,* January 13, 2016, https://hbr.org/2016/01/want-to-be-an-outstanding-leader-keep-a-journal.

8. Researchers have shown that people directed to write short essays about why they had succeeded in a task were more than two times more likely to persist in the face of failure in a subsequent task. See Peter V. Zunick, Russell H. Fazio, and Michael W. Vasey, "Directed Abstraction: Encouraging Broad, Personal Generalizations Following a Success Experience," *Journal of Personality and Social Psychology* 109, no. 1 (2015): 1–19.

CHAPTER 2: LEADERSHIP MAKES A DIFFERENCE

1. This statement has been attributed to Peter Drucker, but in a search of the literature we can find no specific source for it.

2. James Harter and Amy Adkins, "What Great Managers Do to Engage Employees," *Harvard Business Review,* April 2, 2015, https://hbr.org/2015/04/what-great-managers-do-to-engage-employees.

3. We measure engagement by combining responses to these 10 statements: (1) My work group has a strong sense of team spirit; (2) I am proud to tell others that I work for this organization;

(3) I am committed to this organization's success; (4) I would work harder and for longer hours if the job demanded it; (5) I am highly productive in my job; (6) I am clear about what is expected of me in my job; (7) I feel that my organization values my work; (8) I am effective in meeting the demands of my job; (9) Around my workplace, people seem to trust management; and (10) I feel like I am making a difference in this organization. A five-point response scale is used.

4. For more on this, see Barry Z. Posner, *Bringing the Rigor of Research to the Art of Leadership: Evidence Behind The Five Practices of Exemplary Leadership and the LPI: Leadership Practices Inventory* (San Francisco: The Leadership Challenge, A Wiley Brand, 2015), www.leadershipchallenge.com/Research-section-Our-Authors-Research-Detail/bringing-the-rigor-of-research-to-the-art-of-leadership.aspx. Some studies claim that managers account for as much as 70 percent of the variance in employee engagement scores. Some of this, no doubt, is because of differences in how engagement is measured. Still, the point can't be denied that how your leader/manager behaves has a substantial impact on how you feel about your workplace and the energy you put into your work.

5. See, for example, Jonathan Mozingo Wallace, "The Relationship of Leadership Behaviors with Follower Performance: A Study of Alternative Schools" (PhD diss., Regent University, August, 22, 2006).

6. Gregory G. Mader, "Stepping Up to the Plate: Leadership Behavior in Baseball" (Master's thesis, Concordia University, January 2009), 59.

7. Barry Z. Posner, "An Investigation into the Leadership Practices of Volunteer Leaders," *Leadership & Organization Development Journal* 36, no. 7 (2015): 885–898.

8. Barry Z. Posner, "It's How Leaders Behave That Matters, Not Where They Are From," *Leadership & Organization Development Journal* 34, no. 6 (2013): 573–587.

9. Arran Caza and Barry Z. Posner, "Good Leadership Is Universal: Evidence of Global Similarity in the Sources of Followers' Satisfaction with Leaders" (paper presented at the annual meeting of the Western Academy of Management, Kauai, Hawaii, March 2015).

CHAPTER 3: YOU ARE ALREADY LEADING—JUST NOT FREQUENTLY ENOUGH

1. Kouzes, James M., and Barry Z. Posner, *The Leadership Challenge: How to Make Extraordinary Things Happen.* 5th ed. (San Francisco: The Leadership Challenge, A Wiley Brand, 2012).

2. For more information about these studies, you can find abstracts of more than 700 of them on our website: www.theleadershipchallenge .com/research.

3. *The Leadership Challenge* provides a thorough description of this leadership framework, its development, the empirical evidence, and numerous examples and suggestions about how people engage in The Five Practices and is well worth your time to read next in your journey to become the best leader you can be.

4. Kouzes, James M., and Barry Z. Posner, *The Leadership Practices Inventory.* 4th ed. (San Francisco: The Leadership Challenge, A Wiley Brand, 2012).

5. Barry Z. Posner, *Bringing the Rigor of Research to the Art of Leadership: Evidence Behind The Five Practices of Exemplary Leadership and the* LPI: Leadership Practices Inventory (San Francisco: The Leadership Challenge, A Wiley brand, 2015), http://www .leadershipchallenge.com/Research-section-Our-Authors-Research-Detail/bringing-the-rigor-of-research-to-the-art-of-leadership.aspx.

6. Janet Houser, "A Model for Developing the Context of Nursing Care Delivery." *Journal of Nursing Administration* 33, no. 1 (2003): 39–47.

7. Sean Niles Donnelly, "The Roles of Principal Leadership Behaviors and Organizational Routines in Montana's Distinguished Title I Schools" (EdD diss., Montana State University, April, 2012).

8. William F. Maloney, "Project Site Leadership Role in Improving Construction Safety" (unpublished research report, Center for Innovation in Construction Safety and Health Research, Virginia Polytechnic Institute and State University, March 2010).

9. William H. Burton, "Examining the Relationship between Leadership Behaviors of Senior Pastors and Church Growth" (PhD diss., Northcentral University, January 2010).

10. Yueh-Ti Chen, "Relationships among Emotional Intelligence, Cultural Intelligence, Job Performance, and Leader Effectiveness: A

Study of County Extension Directors in Ohio" (PhD diss., The Ohio State University, October 2013).

11. Mary H. Sylvester, "Transformational Leadership Behavior of Frontline Sales Professionals: An Investigation of the Impact of Resilience and Key Demographics" (PhD diss., Capella University, November 2009).

12. JP van der Westhuizen and Andrea Garnett, "The Correlation of Leadership Practices of First and Second Generation Family Business Owners to Business Performance," *Mediterranean Journal of Social Sciences* 5, no. 21 (2014): 27–38.

13. Virginia S. Blair, "Clinical Executive Leadership Behaviors and the Hospital Quality Initiative: Impact on Acute Care Hospitals" (PhD diss., University of Phoenix, November 2008).

14. James M. Kouzes and Barry Z. Posner, *The Truth About Leadership: The No-Fads, Heart-of-the-Matter Facts You Need to Know* (San Francisco: Jossey-Bass, 2010).

CHAPTER 4: YOU HAVE TO BELIEVE IN YOURSELF

1. Our colleague Bob Vanourek shared these stories with us. They're included in his book, *Leadership Wisdom: Lessons from Poetry, Prose, and Curious Verse* (Melbourne, FL: Motivational Press, 2016).

2. Jim Tweedy also paints the "self-portraits" of dogs and other animals. See www.jimtweedy.com for images of the self-portraits (accessed July 11, 2015).

3. Jane Blake is a pseudonym. The story, however, is real and the quote is direct from correspondence with this individual.

4. Michael Hyatt, with Stu McLaren, "Season 4, Episode 12: What if the Barriers Were Only in Your Head? Defeating Limiting Beliefs in the 3 Major Areas of Life," video, 36:50, July 22, 2015, http://michaelhyatt.com/season-4-episode-12-what-if-the-barriers-were-only-in-your-head-podcast.html.

5. Albert Bandura, *Self-Efficacy: The Exercise of Control* (New York: W. H. Freeman, 1997).

6. Robert Wood and Albert Bandura, "Impact of Conceptions of Ability on Self-Regulatory Mechanisms and Complex Decision Making," *Journal of Personality and Social Psychology* 56, no. 3 (1989): 407–415.

7. Albert Bandura and Robert Wood, "Effect of Perceived Controllability and Performance Standards on Self-Regulation of Complex Decision Making," *Journal of Personality and Social Psychology* 56, no. 5 (1989): 805–814.

CHAPTER 5: LEARNING
IS THE MASTER SKILL

1. Daniel T. Willingham, *Why Don't Students Like School? A Cognitive Scientist Answers Questions About How the Mind Works and What It Means for the Classroom* (San Francisco: Jossey-Bass, 2009).

2. Lillas M. Brown and Barry Z. Posner, "Exploring the Relationship Between Learning and Leadership," *Leadership & Organization Development Journal* 22, no. 6 (2001): 274–280. See also Barry Z. Posner, "Understanding the Learning Tactics of College Students and Their Relationship to Leadership," *Leadership & Organization Development Journal* 30, no. 4 (2009): 386–395.

3. David H. Maister, "How's Your Asset?" http://davidmaister.com/articles/hows-your-asset.

4. You can learn more about our programs to develop leadership by visiting our website: www.leadershipchallenge.com/home.aspx.

5. Barry Z. Posner, "A Longitudinal Study Examining Changes in Students' Leadership Behavior," *Journal of College Student Development* 50, no. 5 (2009): 551–563.

6. Carol S. Dweck, *Mindset: The New Psychology of Success* (New York: Random House, 2006). Dweck also writes elsewhere that there are three common misconceptions about a growth mindset: "I already have it, and I always have it"; "A growth mindset is just about praising and rewarding effort"; and, "Just espouse a growth mindset, and good things will happen." See Carol. Dweck, "What Having a 'Growth Mindset' Actually Means," *Harvard Business Review*,

January 13, 2016, https://hbr.org/2016/01/what-having-a-growth-mindset-actually-means.

7. Dweck, *Mindset*, 6.

8. Albert Bandura and Robert Wood, "Effects of Perceived Controllability and Performance Standards on Self-Regulation of Complex Decision Making," *Journal of Personality and Social Psychology* 56, no. 5 (1989): 805–814.

9. See Dweck, *Mindset*, for a discussion of numerous research studies in all these and other domains.

10. *Harvard Business Review* staff, "Talent: How Companies Can Profit from a 'Growth Mindset,'" *Harvard Business Review*, November 2014, https://hbr.org/2014/11/how-companies-can-profit-from-a-growth-mindset.

11. Dweck, *Mindset*, 6. Emphasis in original.

12. Peter A. Heslin, Don Vandwalle, and Gary P. Latham, "Keen to Help? Managers' Implicit Person Theories and Their Subsequent Employee Coaching," *Personnel Psychology* 59, no. 4 (2006): 871–902. See also Francesca Gino and Bradley Staats, "Why Organizations Don't Learn," *Harvard Business Review*, November 2015, https://hbr.org/2015/11/why-organizations-dont-learn.

CHAPTER 6: LEADERSHIP EMERGES FROM WITHIN

1. Anne Lamott, *Bird by Bird: Some Instructions on Writing and Life* (New York: Pantheon, 199–200).

CHAPTER 7: YOU HAVE TO KNOW WHAT'S IMPORTANT TO YOU

1. Barry Z. Posner, "Another Look at the Impact of Personal and Organizational Values Congruency," *Journal of Business Ethics* 97, no. 4 (2010): 535–541.

2. Brian S. Hall, *Values Shift: A Guide to Personal and Organizational Transformation* (Eugene, OR: Wipf & Stock, 2006).

3. Posner, "Another Look"; Barry Z. Posner and Robert I. Westwood, "A Cross-Cultural Investigation of the Shared Values Relationship,"

International Journal of Value-Based Management 11, no. 4 (1995): 1–10; Barry Z. Posner and Warren H. Schmidt, "Demographic Characteristics and Shared Values," *International Journal of Value-Based Management* 5, no. 1 (1992): 77–87; Barry Z. Posner and Warren H. Schmidt, "Values Congruence and Differences Between the Interplay of Personal and Organizational Value Systems," *Journal of Business Ethics* 12, no. 5 (1992): 341–347; Barry Z. Posner, "Individual Characteristics and Shared Values: It Makes No Nevermind" (paper presented at the Academy of Management, Western Division, Salt Lake City, March 1990); and Barry Z. Posner, James M. Kouzes, and Warren H. Schmidt, "Shared Values Make a Difference: An Empirical Test of Corporate Culture," *Human Resource Management* 24, no. 3 (1985): 293–310.

4. Amy Wrzesniewski, Barry Schwartz, Xiangyu Cong, Michael Kane, Audrey Omar, and Thomas Kolditz, "Multiple Types of Motives Don't Multiply the Motivation of West Point Cadets," *Proceedings of the National Academy of Sciences* 111, no. 30 (2014): 10990–10995, doi:10.1073/pnas.140529111.

5. Thomas Kolditz, "Why You Lead Determines How Well You Lead," *Harvard Business Review Blog*, July 2014, https://hbr.org/2014/07/why-you-lead-determines-how-well-you-lead.

CHAPTER 8: WHO YOU ARE ISN'T WHO YOU WILL BE

1. This inquiry is consistent with Marshall Goldsmith with Mark Reiter, *What Got You Here Won't Get You There: How Successful People Become Even More Successful* (New York: Hyperion, 2007).

2. James M. Kouzes and Barry Z. Posner, 2011 *Credibility: How Leaders Gain and Lose It, Why People Demand It,* 2nd ed. (San Francisco: Jossey-Bass, 2011).

3. See also Susie Cranston and Scott Keller, "Increasing the 'Meaning Quotient' of Work," *McKinsey Quarterly*, January 2013.

4. These leadership behaviors are associated with Inspiring a Shared Vision; and among the 30 leadership behaviors measured on the Leadership Practices Inventory, they are typically among the least frequently engaged in.

5. For another discussion of ideal self in leadership, see Richard E. and Kleio Akrivou, "The Ideal Self as the Driver of Intentional Change," *Journal of Management Development* 25, no. 7 (2006): 624–642.

CHAPTER 9: IT'S NOT JUST ABOUT YOU

1. We define *leadership* this way: "Leadership is the art of mobilizing others to want to struggle for shared aspirations." James M. Kouzes and Barry Z. Posner, *The Leadership Challenge: How to Make Extraordinary Things Happen.* 5th ed. (San Francisco: The Leadership Challenge, A Wiley Brand, 2012).

2. See V. I. Sessa and J. J. Taylor, *Executive Selection: Strategies for Success* (San Francisco: Jossey-Bass, 2000). See also Daniel Goleman, *Emotional Intelligence: Why It Can Be More than IQ,* 10th Anniversary ed. (New York: Bantam Dell, 2006); Claudio Fernández-Aráoz, "The Challenge of Hiring Senior Executives," in Cary Cherniss and Daniel Goleman, eds. *The Emotionally Intelligent Workplace (Advances in Emotional Intelligence): How to Select for, Measure, and Improve Emotional Intelligence in Individuals, Groups, and Organizations* (San Francisco: Jossey-Bass, 2001), 189; and Morgan W. McCall and Michael M. Lombardo, *Off the Track: Why and How Successful Executives Get Derailed* (Greensboro, NC: Center for Creative Leadership, 1983).

3. You can access Reverend Dr. Martin Luther King Jr.'s "I Have a Dream" speech at the Lincoln Memorial on YouTube: https://www.youtube.com/watch?v=3vDWWy4CMhE. A printed version of the speech is in Coretta S. King, ed., *The Words of Martin Luther King, Jr.* (New York: Newmarket Press, 1984), 95–98.

4. Universum, "Millennials: Understanding a Misunderstood Generation," 2015, http://universumglobal.com/millennials.

5. Tony Schwartz and Christine Porath, "Why You Hate Work," *New York Times*, May 30, 2014, www.nytimes.com/2014/06/01/opinion/sunday/why-you-hate-work.html?_r=2.

6. David S. Yeager, Marlone D. Henderson, David Paunesku, Gregory G. Walton, Sidney D'Mello, Brian J. Spitzer, and Angela Lee Duckworth, "Boring but Important: A Self-Transcendent Purpose for

Learning Fosters Academic Self-Regulation," *Journal of Personality and Social Psychology* 107, no. 4 (2014): 559–580.

7. Amy Wrzesniewski, Clark McCauey, Paul Rozin, and Barry Schwartz, "Jobs, Careers, and Callings: People's Relations to Their Work," *Journal of Research in Personality* 31, no. 1 (1997): 21–33.

CHAPTER 10: CHALLENGE IS YOUR LEADERSHIP TRAINING GROUND

1. For a discussion of this truth and many others, see James M. Kouzes and Barry Z. Posner, *The Truth About Leadership: The No-Fads, Heart-of-the-Matter Facts You Need to Know* (San Francisco: Jossey-Bass, 2010).
2. Patricia Sellers, "What Happens When the World's Most Powerful Women Get Together," *Fortune*, November 1, 2015, 26.
3. Mihaly Csikszentmihalyi, *Flow: The Psychology of Optimal Experience* (New York: Harper and Row, 1990), 3.
4. These are two of the questions included on the Leadership Practices Inventory.
5. Carnegie Mellon University, "Randy Pausch Last Lecture: Achieving Your Childhood Dreams," YouTube video, 1:16:26, September 18, 2007, https://www.youtube.com/watch?v=ji5_MqicxSo. Also see Randy Pausch, with Jeffrey Zaslow, *The Last Lecture* (New York: Hyperion, 2008).
6. Warren Bennis, *On Becoming a Leader,* 4th ed. (New York: Basic Books, 2009), 146.
7. Executive Development Associates, *EDA Trends in Executive Development 2014: A Benchmark Report* (Oklahoma City, OK: Executive Development Associates and Pearson, 2014), www.executivedevelopment.com/online-solutions/product/trends-in-executive-development-2014/.
8. Sam Davis, "The State of Global Leadership Development," *Training*, July/August 2015, 30–33, www.trainingmag.com/sites/default/files//030_trg0715AMA3.pdf.
9. Too often, when people look at the accomplishments of others, they focus only on the end and don't appreciate the many

struggles, misfortunes, twists of fate, disappointments, and the like they had to go through to reach that end.

CHAPTER 11: GET CURIOUS AND GO KICK THE BALL AROUND

1. For more information on Don Bennett's ascent of Mt. Rainier, see James M. Kouzes and Barry Z. Posner, *The Leadership Challenge: How to Make Extraordinary Things Happen*. 5th ed. (San Francisco: The Leadership Challenge, A Wiley Brand, 2012), 189–190.
2. Thomas S. Bateman and J. Michael Crant, "The Proactive Component of Organizational Behavior: Measures and Correlates," *Journal of Organizational Behavior* 14, no. 2 (1993): 103–118. See also Barry Z. Posner and Joseph W. Harder, "The Proactive Personality, Leadership, Gender and National Culture" (paper presented at the Western Academy of Management, Santa Fe, NM, March 2002).
3. J. Michael Crant, "The Proactive Personality Scale and Objective Job Performance among Real Estate Agents," *Journal of Applied Psychology* 80, no. 4 (1995): 532–537.
4. Jeffery A. Thompson, "Proactive Personality and Job Performance: A Social Capital Perspective," *Journal of Applied Psychology* 90, no. 5 (2005): 1011–1017.
5. Brian Grazer and Charles Fishman, *A Curious Mind: The Secret to a Bigger Life* (New York: Simon & Schuster, 2015), xii.
6. Ibid.
7. Ibid., 188–189.
8. Ibid., 260.
9. J. K. Rowling, *Very Good Lives: The Fringe Benefits of Failure and Importance of Imagination* (New York: Little, Brown, 2008), 34.
10. James M. Kouzes and Barry Z. Posner, *The Leadership Challenge,* 4th ed. (San Francisco: Jossey-Bass, 2007), 194–195.
11. If you need help coming up with ideas, you'll find lots of them in this book, which is organized around the 30 leadership behaviors: James M. Kouzes and Barry Z. Posner, with Elaine Biech, *A Coach's Guide to Developing Exemplary Leaders: Making the Most of* The Leadership Challenge *and the* Leadership Practices Inventory *(LPI)* (San Francisco: Pfeiffer, 2010).

CHAPTER 12: GET GRITTY
AND STAY HARDY

1. Angela Lee Duckworth, "The Key to Success? Grit," TED, May 2013, www.ted.com/talks/angela_lee_duckworth_the_key_to_success_grit/transcript?language=en.

2. Angela Lee Duckworth, Christopher Peterson, Michael D. Matthews, and Dennis R. Kelly, "Personality Processes and Individual Differences: Grit: Perseverance and Passion for Long-Term Goals," *Journal of Personality and Social Psychology* 92, no. 6 (2007): 1087–1088.

3. For example, see Lauren Eskrieis-Winkler, Elizabeth P. Shulman, Scott A. Beal, and Angela Lee Duckworth, "The Grit Effect: Predicting Retention in the Military, the Workplace, School, and Marriage," *Frontiers in Psychology* 5, no. 36 (2014): 1–12; Angela Lee Duckworth, Patrick D. Quinn, and Martin E. P. Seligman, "Positive Predictors of Teacher Effectiveness," *Journal of Positive Psychology* 4, no. 6 (2009): 540–547; and Angela Lee Duckworth, Teri A. Kirbyu, Eli Tsukayama, Heather Berstein, and K. Anders Ericsson, "Deliberate Practice Spells Success: Why Grittier Competitors Triumph at the National Spelling Bee," *Social Psychology & Personality Science* 2, no. 2 (2011): 174–181.

4. Yahoo! Sports, "Sky the Limit for Towering Knicks Rookie Porzingis," December 2015, http://sports.yahoo.com/news/sky-the-limit-for-towering-knicks-rookie-porzingis-215200553.html.

5. Laura W. Geller, "Angela Duckworth's Gritty View of Success," *Strategy+Business* (Spring 2014): 15–17.

6. Duckworth, "Key to Success?"

7. Salvatore R. Maddi, Michael D. Matthews, Dennis R. Kelly, Brandilynn Villarreal, and Marina White, "The Role of Hardiness and Grit in Predicting Performance and Retention of USMA Cadets," *Military Psychology* 24, no. 1 (2012): 19–28; John P. Meriac, John S. Slifka, and Lauren R. LaBat, "Work Ethic and Grit: An Examination of Empirical Redundancy," *Personality and Individual Differences* 86 (2015): 401–405.

8. For a history of the research on psychological hardiness, see Salvatore R. Maddi, "The Story of Hardiness: Twenty Years of Theorizing, Research, and Practice," *Consulting Psychology Journal: Practices*

and Research 54, no. 3 (2002): 175–185. Also see Salvatore R. Maddi and Suzanne C. Kobasa. 1984. *The Hardy Executive: Health Under Stress* (Chicago: Dorsey Professional Books, 1984); and Salvatore R. Maddi and Deborah M. Khoshaba, *Resilience at Work: How to Succeed No Matter What Life Throws at You* (New York: AMACOM, 2005).

9. See Reginald A. Bruce and Robert F. Sinclair, "Exploring the Psychological Hardiness of Entrepreneurs," *Frontiers of Entrepreneurship Research* 29, no. 6 (2009): n.p.; Paul T. Bartone, Robert R. Roland, James J. Picano, and Thomas J. Williams, "Psychological Hardiness Predicts Success in US Army Special Forces Candidates," *International Journal of Selection and Assessment* 16, no. 1 (2008): 78–81; and Paul T. Bartone, "Resilience Under Military Operational Stress: Can Leaders Influence Hardiness?" *Military Psychology* 18 (2006): S141–S148.

10. Maddi et al., "Role of Hardiness."

11. Fred Luthans, Gretchen R. Vogelgesang, and Paul B. Lester, "Developing the Psychological Capital of Resiliency," *Human Resource Development Review* 5, no. 1 (2006): 25–44.

12. Martin E. P. Seligman, "Building Resilience," *Harvard Business Review*, April 2011, 101–106.

13. Seligman, "Building Resilience," 102.

14. We talk about this more in James M. Kouzes and Barry Z. Posner, *Turning Adversity Into Opportunity* (San Francisco: Jossey-Bass, 2014).

15. Barbara L. Fredrickson, *Positivity: Groundbreaking Research Reveals How to Embrace the Hidden Strength of Positive Emotions, Overcome Negativity, and Thrive* (New York: Crown, 2009).

16. See, for example, Amit Sood, *The Mayo Clinic Guide to Stress-Free Living* (Boston: Da Capo Press, 2013).

CHAPTER 13: COURAGE GIVES YOU THE STRENGTH TO GROW

1. We write more about courage and the role it plays for leadership in our book *A Leader's Legacy* (San Francisco: Jossey-Bass, 2006). See also Bill Treasurer, *Courage Goes to Work: How to Build Backbones, Boost Performance, and Get Results* (San Francisco: Berrett-Koehler Publishers, 2008).

2. Eleanor Roosevelt, *You Learn by Living: Eleven Keys for a More Fulfilling Life,* 50th anniversary ed (New York: Harper Perennial, 2011), 29–30.

3. It may be useful to distinguish somewhat between bravery and courage, largely in terms of their relationship to fear. Bravery, on the one hand, has to do with the ability to confront pain, danger, hardships, and the like without any feelings of fear. Courage, on the other hand, is the ability to act despite feelings of fear. More than bravery, courage is a state of mind that motivates action fueled by a cause that makes the struggle worthwhile. In this sense, courage is more mindful than bravery, requiring critical judgement about what you are getting yourself into and why this matters, whereas bravery is generally an inherent characteristic that doesn't involve much conscious thought. These days, however, these two terms are often used interchangeably.

4. In one study 243 of the 250 participants answered the question "How could you have responded to that situation in a NONcourageous manner?" by indicating that they could have taken an alternative, often easier, action. Cynthia L. S. Pury, Robin M. Kowalski, and Jana Spearman, "Distinctions between General and Personal Courage," *Journal of Positive Psychology* 2, no. 2 (2007): 99–114.

5. For example, see Shawn Achor, *Before Happiness: The 5 Hidden Keys to Achieving Success, Spreading Happiness, and Sustaining Positive Change* (New York: Crown Business, 2013).

6. Quoted in Margie Warrell, *Stop Playing Safe: Rethink Risk. Unlock the Power of Courage. Achieve Outstanding Success* (Melbourne, Australia: John Wiley & Sons, 2013), 232.

7. Warrell, *Stop Playing Safe*, 232.

8. Ibid.

9. Quoted in Warrell, *Stop Playing Safe*, 232.

10. In our teaching, training, and coaching, we use the *Leadership Practices Inventory* as our tool for assessing and providing feedback on leader behaviors. See James M. Kouzes and Barry Z. Posner, *Leadership Practices Inventory,* 4th ed. (San Francisco: Pfeiffer, 2012).

11. Cynthia L. S. Pury, C. Starkey, W. Hawkins, L. Weber, and S. Saylors, "A Cognitive Appraisal Model of Courage" (paper presented at the First World Congress on Positive Psychology, Philadelphia, June 2009).

CHAPTER 14: I COULDN'T HAVE DONE IT WITHOUT YOU

1. Red Bull, "Red Bull Air Race," accessed November 21, 2015, www.redbullairrace.com/en_US.
2. For a revealing and personal look at these issues, especially applied to doctors, see Atul Gawande, "Personal Best: Top Athletes and Singers Have Coaches. Should You?" *New Yorker*, October 3, 2011, www.newyorker.com/magazine/2011/10/03/personal-best.
3. Scott Barry Kaufman, "Which Character Strengths Are Most Predictive of Well-Being?" *Beautiful Minds* (blog), August 2, 2015, http:// blogs.scientificamerican.com/beautiful-minds/which-character-strengths-are-most-predictive-of-well-being.
4. Brandon Busteed, "The Two Most Important Questions for Graduates," Gallup, June 12, 2015, www.gallup.com/opinion/ gallup/183599/two-important-questions-graduates.aspx.
5. Benjamin S. Bloom, ed., *Developing Talent in Young People* (New York: Ballantine Books, 1985), 3.
6. George E. Vaillant, *Triumphs of Experience: The Men of the Harvard Grant Study* (Cambridge, MA: Belknap Press, 2012), 27. See also Joshua Wolf Shenk, "What Makes Us Happy?" *The Atlantic*, June 2009, www.theatlantic.com/magazine/print/2009/06/ what-makes-us-happy/7439.
7. Richard D. Cotton, Yan Shen, and Reut Livne-Tarandach, "On Becoming Extraordinary: The Content and Structure of the Developmental Networks of Major League Baseball Hall of Famers," *Academy of Management Journal* 54, no. 1 (2011): 15–46.
8. Leigh Gallagher and Daniel Roberts, "The Best Advice I Ever Got," *Fortune*, October 1, 2015, 109.
9. Francis J. Flynn and Vanessa K. B. Lake, "If You Need Help, Just Ask: Underestimating Compliance with Direct Requests for Help," *Journal of Personality and Social Psychology* 95, no. 1 (2008): 128–143.
10. Allison Wood Brooks, Francesca Gino, and Maurice E. Schweitzer, "Smart People Ask for (My) Help: Seeking Advice Boosts Perceptions of Competence," *Management Science* 61, no. 6 (2015): 1431, http://dx.doi.org/10.1287/mnsc.2014.2054. Emphasis in original.

11. Ernest J. Wilson, III, "Empathy Is Still Lacking in the Leaders Who Need It Most," *Harvard Business Review Blog*, September 21, 2015, https://hbr.org/2015/09/empathy-is-still-lacking-in-the-leaders-who-need-it-most. He also reports: "According to an unpublished survey of our graduates over the past 10 years who now occupy professional positions, empathy is most lacking among middle managers and senior executives: the very people who need it most because their actions affect such large numbers of people."

12. Geoff Colvin, *Humans Are Underrated: What High Achievers Know That Brilliant Machines Never Will* (New York: Portfolio, 2015), 49.

CHAPTER 15: GET CONNECTED

1. Here are some other representative comments: "I learned by doing, and making a lot of mistakes," "Good and bad experiences," "Seeking challenging assignments in my career," "Trying new techniques and seeing what works," and "Practice makes perfect—I have learned from trying and succeeding and trying and failing."

2. Other typical comments are "Tried to emulate others that I respect," "From mentors," "Observing managers and identifying what works and what doesn't," "Watching others and acting as I wished they had led me," "By seeking advice and guidance from leaders I respect," "By modeling great leaders," and "Observe others; every situation has something for me to learn."

3. Susan Cain argues that people undervalue introverts and that we lose out because of that. See her book for rich stories about real introverts who were extraordinary leaders: Susan Cain, *Quiet: The Power of Introverts in a World That Can't Stop Talking* (New York: Broadway Books, 2013). Also see the website www.quietrev.com for more stories about introverted leaders.

4. Brian Grazer and Charles Fishman, *A Curious Mind: The Secret to a Bigger Life* (New York: Simon & Schuster, 2015), 22.

5. For a detailed discussion of social capital, see Robert D. Putnam, *Bowling Alone: The Collapse and Revival of American Community* (New York: Simon & Schuster, 2001). Also see Malcolm Gladwell, *The Tipping Point: How Little Things Can Make a Big Difference* (Boston: Back Bay Books, 2002). For a practical application of

social capital research to the world of business, see Wayne E. Baker, *Achieving Success Through Social Capital: Tapping the Hidden Resources in Your Personal and Business Networks,* University of Michigan Business Management Series (San Francisco: Jossey-Bass, 2000).

6. See, for example, Matthew D. Lieberman, *Social: Why Our Brains Are Wired to Connect* (New York: Crown Publishers, 2013) and Frans de Waal, *The Age of Empathy: Nature's Lessons for a Kinder Society* (New York: Three Rivers Press, 2009). Also see Nicholas A. Christakis and James M. Fowler, *Connected: How Your Friends' Friends' Friends Affect Everything You Feel, Think, and Do* (Boston: Back Bay Books, 2011).

7. James M. Citrin, "What Parents Should Tell Their Kids About Finding a Career," *Harvard Business Review Blog*, May 15, 2015, https://hbr.org/2015/05/what-parents-should-tell-their-kids-about-finding-a-career.

8. Cheryl L. Carmichael, Harry T. Reis, and Paul R. Duberstein, "In Your 20s It's Quantity, in Your 30s It's Quality: The Prognostic Values of Social Activity across 30 Years of Adulthood," *Psychology and Aging* 30, no. 1 (2015): 95–105.

9. Jane E. Dutton, "Build High-Quality Connections," in *How to Be a Positive Leader: Small Actions, Big Impact*, ed. Jane E. Dutton and Gretchen Spreitzer (San Francisco: Berrett-Koehler Publishers, 2014), 11–21.

10. Unlike a corporate board, your personal board doesn't have to meet together. For some people, however, the chance for them to interact with like-minded, talented individuals may be a reason why they'd like to be on your board.

CHAPTER 16: WITHOUT FEEDBACK YOU CANNOT GROW

1. For an overview of this effect, see Vera Hoorens, "Self-Enhancement and Superiority Biases in Social Comparisons," *European Review of Social Psychology* 4, no. 1 (1993): 113–139, doi:10.1080/14792779343000040. Such findings have also been found in non-Western cultures; for example, see Jonathon D. Brown and Chihiro Kobayashi, "Self-Enhancement in Japan and America," *Asian Journal of Social Psychology* 5 (2002): 145–167.

2. K. Patricia Cross, "Not Can, but *Will* College Teaching Be Improved?" *New Directions for Higher Education* 17 (1977): 1–15.

3. Allstate, "New Allstate Survey Shows Americans Think They Are Great Drivers—Habits Tell a Different Story," November 3, 2011, www.allstatenewsroom.com/channels/News-Releases/releases/new-allstate-survey-shows-americans-think-they-are-great-drivers-habits-tell-a-different-story-6/.

4. David M. Messick, Suzanne Bloom, Janet P. Boldizar, and Charles D. Samuelson, "Why We Are Fairer than Others," *Journal of Experimental Social Psychology* 21, no. 5 (1985): 480–500.

5. Erich C. Dierdorff and Robert S. Rubin, "Research: We're Not Very Self-Aware, Especially at Work," *Harvard Business Review Blog*, March 14, 2015, https://hbr.org/2015/03/research-were-not-very-self-aware-especially-at-work.

6. Barry Z. Posner, "Understanding the Learning Tactics of College Students and Their Relationship to Leadership," *Leadership & Organization Development Journal* 30, no. 4 (2009): 386–395; Lillas M. Brown and Barry Z. Posner, "Exploring the Relationship Between Learning and Leadership," *Leadership & Organization Development Journal* 22, no. 6 (2001): 274–280.

7. James M. Kouzes and Barry Z. Posner, "To Get Honest Feedback, Leaders Need to Ask," *Harvard Business Review Blog*, February 27, 2014, https://hbr.org/2014/02/to-get-honest-feedback-leaders-need-to-ask.

8. James M. Kouzes and Barry Z. Posner, *The Leadership Practices Inventory*, 4th ed. (San Francisco: Pfeiffer, 2012).

9. For the record, this statement also has the highest variance or greatest difference of opinion, from the perspectives of both leaders (self) and observers of any of the 30 leadership behaviors on the LPI.

10. Douglas Stone and Sheila Heen, *Thanks for the Feedback: The Science and Art of Receiving Feedback Well* (New York: Penguin Group, 2014).

11. Jack Zenger and Joseph Folkman, "Your Employees Want the Negative Feedback You Hate to Give," *Harvard Business Review Blog*, January 2014, http://blogs.hbr.org/2014/01/your-employees-want-the-negative-feedback-you-hate-to-give.

12. Stone and Heen, *Thanks for the Feedback*, 196–197.

13. We've use a pseudonym here out of respect for the untimely and tragic death of this colleague and leader. His experience and leadership actions are accurate.

14. John W. Gardner, "Uncritical Lovers—Unloving Critics" (commencement speech presented at Cornell University, Ithaca, NY, June 1, 1968).

CHAPTER 17: LEADERSHIP TAKES PRACTICE, AND PRACTICE TAKES TIME

1. James Clear, "Lesson on Success and Deliberate Practice from Mozart, Picasso, and Kobe Bryant," June 9, 2015, http://jamesclear .com/deliberate-practice.

2. K. Anders Ericsson, Michael J. Prietula, and Edward T. Cokely, "The Making of an Expert," *Harvard Business Review*, July/August 2007, 3.

3. Cal Newport, *So Good They Can't Ignore You: Why Skills Trump Passion in the Quest for Work You Love* (New York: Grand Central Publishing, 2012), 33.

4. Piers Steel, *The Procrastination Equation: How to Stop Putting Things Off and Start Getting Stuff Done* (New York: HarperCollins, 2011), 129.

5. This number was popularized by Malcolm Gladwell, *Outliers: The Story of Success* (New York: Little, Brown, 2008). The original research on deliberate practice was done by K. Anders Ericsson, professor of psychology, Florida State University. See K. Anders Ericsson, "The Influence of Experience and Deliberate Practice on the Development of Superior Expert Performance," in *The Cambridge Handbook of Expertise and Expert Performance*, ed. K. Anders Ericsson, Neil Charness, Paul J. Feltovich, and Robert R. Hoffman (New York: Cambridge University Press, 2006), 683–704.

6. George Leonard, *Mastery: The Keys to Success and Long-Term Fulfillment* (New York: Plume, 1992), 19.

7. Active listening is a structured way of responding that requires you to briefly restate the key points the speaker makes and to check with the speaker to ensure that you are hearing him or her accurately.

8. Ericsson, Prietula, and Cokely, "Making of an Expert," 3.

9. Quoted in Michael Jordan and Jonathan Hock, *Michael Jordan to the Max*, DVD, directed by Don Kempf and James D. Stern, Giant Screen Films, Evanston, Illinois, 2000.

10. Brian Brim, "Debunking Strengths Myth #1," *Gallup*, October 11, 2007, www.gallup.com/businessjournal/101665/Debunking-

Strengths-Myths.aspx?g_source=Debunking%20Strengths%20Myth%
20#1&g_medium=search&g_campaign=tiles.

11. One of the improvement tips from Daniel Coyle, who has studied practice extensively, inspired this idea. See Daniel Coyle, *The Little Book of Talent: 52 Tips for Improving Your Skills* (New York: Bantam Books, 2012), 45. For a report on his research on deep practice, see Daniel Coyle, *The Talent Code: Greatness Isn't Born. It's Grown. Here's How* (New York: Bantam Books, 2009).

CHAPTER 18: CONTEXT MATTERS

1. We are using the term *context* the way Harvard professor of psychology Ellen Langer describes it. For a detailed discussion of context as Ellen describes it, see Ellen J. Langer, *Mindfulness,* 25th anniversary ed. (Boston: Da Capo Press, 2014), 37–43. For our purposes, *context* is synonymous with *environment.*

2. Art Kleiner, "Ellen Langer on the Value of Mindfulness in Business," *Strategy+Business*, February 9, 2015, www.strategy-business.com/article/00310?gko=73023&cid=TL20150219&utm_campaign=TL20150219.

3. Langer, *Mindfulness*, 81. You can read about other fascinating experiments in Ellen J. Langer, *Counterclockwise: Mindful Health and the Power of Possibility* (New York: Ballantine Books, 2009).

4. Edgar H. Schein, *Organizational Culture and Leadership,* 4th ed. (San Francisco: Jossey-Bass, 2010), 24. Schein's formal definition of *culture* is: "The culture of a group can be defined as a pattern of shared basic assumptions that the group learned as it solved its problems of external adaptation and internal integration, that has worked well enough to be considered valid and, therefore, to be taught to new members as the correct way to perceive, think, and feel in relation to those problems" (Schein, 2010, p. 18).

5. Senn Delaney. N.d. *Why Fostering a Growth Mindset in Organizations Matters.* 2014. Accessed March 12, 2016. http://knowledge.senndelaney.com/docs/thought_papers/pdf/stanford_agilitystudy_hart.pdf.

6. This survey was done at *The Leadership Challenge Forum,* June 18, 2015, and involved 225 leadership educators, trainers, and coaches.

7. Aon, *Aon Hewitt Top Companies for Leaders: Research Highlights 2015*, accessed February 6, 2016, www.aon.com/

human-capital-consulting/thought-leadership/talent/aon-hewitt-top-companies-for-leaders-highlights-report.jsp. The Hay Group's surveys similarly find that "The Best Companies for Leadership take a more proactive, structured approach to developing people." See Hay Group, *Best Companies for Leadership 2014: Executive Summary,* 2014, https://www.haygroup.com/bestcompaniesforleadership/downloads/Best_Companies_for_Leadership_2014_Executive_summary.pdf.

8. Sarah Houle and Kevin Campbell, "What High-Quality Job Candidates Look for in a Company," Gallup, January 4, 2016, www.gallup.com/businessjournal/187964/high-quality-job-candidates-look-company.aspx.

9. Matthias J. Guber, Bernard D. Gelman, and Charan Ranganath, "States of Curiosity Modulate Hippocampus-Dependent Learning via the Dopaminergic Circuit," *Neuron* 84, no. 2 (2014): 486–496.

10. Adam Bryant, "Jan Singer of Spanx: Using Votes to Guide a Group," Corner Office, *New York Times,* September 26, 2015, www.nytimes.com/2015/09/27/business/jan-singer-of-spanx-using-votes-to-guide-a-group.html?ref=business.

11. You can take a free trial of Leadership Practices Inventory–Self by going to www.leadershipchallenge.com/lpi-trial.aspx.

CHAPTER 19: LEARNING LEADERSHIP MUST BE A DAILY HABIT

1. Jim Whittaker, *A Life on the Edge: Memoirs of Everest and Beyond,* 50th anniversary ed. (Seattle: Mountaineers Books, 2013), 16.

2. Harry M. Jansen Kraemer Jr., *From Values to Action: The Four Principles of Values-Based Leadership* (San Francisco: Jossey-Bass, 2011), 15.

3. Harry M. Jansen Kraemer Jr., *Becoming the Best: Build a World-Class Organization Through Values-Based Leadership* (Hoboken, NJ: John Wiley & Sons, 2015), 12.

4. Lewis Howes, *The School of Greatness: A Real-World Guide to Living Bigger, Loving Deeper, and Leaving a Legacy* (New York: Rodale, 2015). Emphasis in original.

5. Howes, *School of Greatness,* 161.

6. Ibid., 163–164.

7. Charles Duhigg, *The Power of Habit: Why We Do What We Do in Life and in Business* (New York: Random House, 2012), 19.

8. Duhigg, *Power of Habit*, 62. In the book's appendix, "A Reader's Guide to Using These Ideas," 275–286, there is useful guidance on how to experiment with ways to change or develop habits.

9. Gretchen Rubin, *Better Than Before: Mastering the Habits of Our Everyday Lives* (New York: Crown Publishers, 2015), xi.

10. Teresa Amabile and Steven Kramer, *The Progress Principle: Using Small Wins to Ignite Joy, Engagement, and Creativity at Work* (Boston: Harvard Business Review Press, 2011).

11. Marshall Goldsmith and Mark Reiter, *Triggers: Creating Behavior That Lasts—Becoming the Person You Want to Be* (New York: Crown Business, 2015), 103.

12. Goldsmith and Reiter, *Triggers*, 103.

13. Ibid., 109–110.

CHAPTER 20: IT'S NOT HOW YOU START; IT'S HOW YOU FINISH

1. James M. Kouzes, and Barry Z. Posner, *Credibility: How Leaders Gain and Lose It, Why People Demand It,* 2nd ed. (San Francisco: Jossey-Bass, 2011).

2. Teresa Amabile and Steven J. Kramer, "The Power of Small Wins," *Harvard Business Review*, May 2011, https://hbr.org/2011/05/the-power-of-small-wins. For more extensive treatment of this subject, see Teresa Amabile and Steven Kramer, *The Progress Principle: Using Small Wins to Ignite Joy, Engagement, and Creativity at Work* (Boston: Harvard Business Review Press, 2011).

3. Amabile and Kramer, "Power of Small Wins."

4. Max H. Bazerman and Margaret A. Neale, *Negotiating Rationally* (New York: Free Press, 1992).

5. C. R. Snyder, *The Psychology of Hope: You Can Get Here from There* (New York: Free Press, 2003), 5.

6. Snyder, *Psychology of Hope*, 5–12.

7. Ibid., 25.

ACKNOWLEDGMENTS

In publishing it's traditional to call the section of the book in which authors thank everyone "Acknowledgments." But *acknowledgment* doesn't adequately express our sentiments. *Gratitude* is a much better word to describe what we feel as we reflect on all those who were part of this undertaking. Gratitude captures the spirit of how thankful and appreciative we are to the very talented, hardworking, and inspiring people with whom we collaborated. They encouraged, supported, coached, enlightened, and enabled us.

First on our list are the 10 young leaders who reviewed each chapter of the manuscript and gave us invaluable feedback about both what they liked and what they thought needed improvement. We've dedicated this book to them, and we want to thank them again for all the ways in which they have helped us. They are Travis Carrigan, Amanda Crowell, Abby Donahue, Garrett Jensen, Amelia Klawon, David Klawon, Armeen Komeili, Nick Lopez, Amanda Posner, and William J. Stribling.

A hallmark of all our work is the collection of genuine stories about real leaders, and we continued this distinctiveness in

Learning Leadership. There are more than 40 individuals mentioned in this book, and we want to express our gratitude to (more than simply acknowledge) them for sharing with us, and with you, their experiences and the lessons they've learned. Their examples bring to life the principles and fundamentals we describe in this book.

We continue to be grateful to the talented people we collaborate with from our publisher, John Wiley & Sons, starting with Jeanenne Ray, our editor, who guided this manuscript from the editorial process through to production. It never would have gotten into your hands without her. Judy Howarth was our developmental and copy editor, and her craftsmanship and guidance brought clarity and focus to our writing. Heather Brosius skillfully guided the manuscript through the editorial process, and our publicist, Sadhika Salariya, enabled us to get the key messages out to our readership. We also want to continue expressing our gratitude for being able to work with Marisa Kelley, product manager, Workplace Learning Solutions, for her ongoing support in expanding the global reach of *The Leadership Challenge* brand. We offer a special shout-out to Matt Holt, publisher, and Shannon Vargo, associate publisher, for being at the helm to steer us through the rough seas of change in the publishing business.

High fives to other members of *The Leadership Challenge* team at Wiley: Eli Becker, Michael Damore, Aneesa Davenport, Michael Friedberg, William Hull, Alison Knowles, Lesley Lura, Kathy Niebenhaus, and David Palmer. We remain always grateful for the expertise and generosity of the best team in this business.

Research and writing take time—time to think, reflect, write, revise, and edit and then think, reflect, write, revise, and edit again. This is precious time we steal from our awesome spouses; and still they are always with us, sometimes urging us on, sometimes telling us it's time to take a break, and very often adding exceptional ideas from their own professional experiences that make the work much better. We express our deepest gratitude to Tae Kyung Kouzes and Jackie Schmidt-Posner for their love, encouragement, sacrifices, and graciousness. They are our coaches, mentors, best friends, and generous supporters without whom we would never be able to write a word.

ABOUT THE AUTHORS

Jim Kouzes and Barry Posner have been working together for more than 30 years, studying leaders, researching leadership, conducting leadership development seminars, and serving as leaders themselves in various capacities. They are coauthors of the award-winning, best-selling book *The Leadership Challenge*, now in its fifth edition. Since its first edition in 1987, *The Leadership Challenge* has sold more than 2 million copies worldwide, and it is available in 21 languages. It has won numerous awards, including the Critics' Choice Award from the nation's book review editors and the James A. Hamilton Hospital Administrators' Book of the Year Award; has been named a Best Business Book of the Year (2012) by *Fast Company*; and was selected as one of the top 10 books on leadership in Jack Covert and Todd Sattersten's *The 100 Best Business Books of All Time*.

Jim and Barry have coauthored more than a dozen other award-winning leadership books, including *The Truth About Leadership: The No-Fads, Heart-of-the-Matter Facts You Need to Know*; *Credibility: How Leaders Gain and Lose It, Why People Demand It*; *Encouraging the Heart: A Leader's Guide to*

Rewarding and Recognizing Others; *A Leader's Legacy*; *The Student Leadership Challenge*; *Extraordinary Leadership in Australia and New Zealand: The Five Practices That Create Great Workplaces* (with Michael Bunting); *Turning Adversity into Opportunity*; *Finding the Courage to Lead*; *Great Leadership Creates Great Workplaces*; *Making Extraordinary Things Happen in Asia: Applying The Five Practices of Exemplary Leadership* (with Steve DeKrey); and *The Academic Administrator's Guide to Exemplary Leadership.*

They also developed the highly acclaimed *Leadership Practices Inventory (LPI)*, a 360-degree questionnaire for assessing leadership behavior, which is one of the most widely used leadership assessment instruments in the world. More than 700 research studies, doctoral dissertations, and academic papers have used The Five Practices of Exemplary Leadership framework they developed.

Jim and Barry have received the Association for Talent Development's highest award for their Distinguished Contribution to Workplace Learning and Performance. In addition, they have been named Management/Leadership Educators of the Year by the International Management Council, ranked by *Leadership Excellence* magazine in the top 20 on its list of the Top 100 Thought Leaders, named among the 50 Top Coaches in the United States (according to *Coaching for Leadership*), ranked as Top 100 Thought Leaders in Trustworthy Business Behavior by Trust Across America, listed among *HR* magazine's Most Influential International Thinkers, and included among the list of today's Top 50 Leadership Thinkers by *Inc.* magazine.

Jim and Barry are frequent keynote speakers, and each has conducted numerous leadership development programs for corporate and for-purpose organizations around the globe. These include Alberta Health Services, ANZ Bank, Apple, Applied Materials, Association of California Nurse Leaders, AT&T, Australia

Institute of Management, Australia Post, Bain Capital, Bank of America, Bose, Camp Fire USA, Charles Schwab, Chevron, Cisco Systems, Clorox, Conference Board of Canada, Consumers Energy, Deloitte & Touche, Dow Chemical, EMQ Families First, Egon Zehnder, Electronic Arts, FedEx, Genentech, Google, Gymboree, Hewlett-Packard, IBM, IKEA, jobsDB Singapore, Johnson & Johnson, Kaiser Foundation Health Plans and Hospitals, Korean Management Association, Intel, Itaú Unibanco, L.L.Bean, Lawrence Livermore National Laboratory, Lockheed Martin, Lucile Packard Children's Hospital, Merck, Monsanto, Motorola, National Head Start Association, Nationwide Insurance, NetApp, Northrop Grumman, Novartis, Nvidia, Oracle, Petronas, Pixar, Roche Bioscience, Telstra, Siemens, Silicon Valley Bank, 3M, Texas Medical Center, TIAA-CREF, Toyota, United Way, Universal Orlando, USAA, Verizon, Visa, Vodafone, Walt Disney Company, Western Mining Corporation, and Westpac. They have lectured at more than 60 college and university campuses.

Jim Kouzes is the Dean's Executive Fellow of Leadership, Leavey School of Business at Santa Clara University, and lectures on leadership around the world to corporations, governments, and nonprofits. He is a highly regarded leadership scholar and an experienced executive; the *Wall Street Journal* cited him as one of the 12 best executive educators in the United States. In 2010, Jim received the Thought Leadership Award from the Instructional Systems Association, the most prestigious award given by the trade association of training and development industry providers. He was listed as one of *HR* magazine's Most Influential International Thinkers for 2010 through 2012, named one of the 2010 through 2016 Top 100 Thought Leaders in Trustworthy Business Behavior by Trust Across America and honored as one of its Lifetime Achievement recipients in 2015, cited by the Association of Corporate Executive Coaches as the 2015 International Executive Coach Thought Leader of Distinction, and selected by Global Gurus as one of the Top 30 Leadership Gurus in 2015. In 2006, Jim was presented with the Golden Gavel, the highest honor awarded by Toastmasters International. Jim served as president, CEO, and chairman of the Tom Peters Company from 1988 through 2000 and prior to that led the Executive Development Center at Santa Clara University (1981–1988). Jim founded the Joint Center for Human Services Development at San Jose State University (1972–1980) and was on the staff of the School of Social Work, University of Texas. His career in training and development began in 1969 when he conducted seminars for Community Action Agency staff and volunteers in the war on poverty. Following graduation from Michigan State University (BA degree with honors in political science), he served as a Peace Corps volunteer (1967–1969). Jim can be reached at jim@kouzes.com.

Barry Posner is the Accolti Endowed Professor of Leadership at the Leavey School of Business, Santa Clara University, where he served as dean of the school for 12 years. He has been a distinguished visiting professor at Hong Kong University of Science and Technology, Sabanci University (Istanbul), and the University of Western Australia. At Santa Clara he has received the President's Distinguished Faculty Award, the School's Extraordinary Faculty Award, and several other teaching and academic honors. Barry has been named one of his nation's top management/leadership educators by the International Management Council, recognized as one of the Top 50 leadership coaches in America and Top 100 Thought Leaders in Trustworthy Business Behavior, ranked among the Most Influential HR Thinkers in the world, and listed among the Top Leadership and Management Experts in the world by *Inc.* magazine. An internationally renowned scholar and educator, Barry has authored or coauthored more than 100 research and practitioner-focused articles. He currently serves on the editorial advisory board for *Leadership & Organizational Development Journal* and the *International Journal of Servant-Leadership* and received the Outstanding Scholar Award for Career Achievement from the *Journal of Management Inquiry.*

Barry received his BA with honors in political science from the University of California, Santa Barbara; his MA in public administration from The Ohio State University; and his PhD in organizational behavior and administrative theory from the University of Massachusetts Amherst. Having consulted with a wide variety of public and private sector organizations worldwide, Barry also works at a strategic level with a number of community-based and professional organizations. He has served on the board of directors of EMQ FamiliesFirst, the Global Women's Leadership Network, American Institute of Architects (AIA), Big Brothers/Big Sisters of Santa Clara County, Center for Excellence in Nonprofits, Junior Achievement of Silicon Valley and Monterey Bay, Public Allies, San Jose Repertory Theater, Sigma Phi Epsilon Fraternity, as well as publicly traded and start-up companies. Barry can be reached at bposner@scu.edu.

INDEX